TALES
FROM AN
ADIRONDACK COUNTY

TALES

FROM AN

ADIRONDACK
COUNTY

TED ABER
AND
STELLA KING

1981
PROSPECT BOOKS
BOX 57
PROSPECT, NEW YORK 13435

First Printing 1961
Second Printing 1978
Third Printing 1981

ISBN 0-913710-07-5

To
the People, Past and Present,
of Hamilton County,
with Deep Admiration and
Profound Respect

CONTENTS

ILLUSTRATIONS

FOREWORD

No work that seeks to tell the stories of a people can ever be the work of the authors alone. It was the people of the Central Adirondacks who wrote the stories. It was the people who passed them to the younger generations. Such legend is the product of individuals, past and present, who have known the region best. Together, their stories form the composite picture of a segment of civilization. Together, they represent the work of all who live within the mountains' steadfast depths.

The list of those who contributed, in large measure or small, to the present work, would fill almost as many pages as their stories. Many have already gone, leaving their legends behind. Those who live are repeating the experiences of youth or the stories told them by parents and grandparents in years long past.

Yet special acknowledgment is due those who willingly gave of their time, their memories, and their knowledge that the legends of an unusual area might remain. Among these are:

ARIETTA AND PISECO:
William Baker, Mr. and Mrs. Kenneth Hansen, Mr. and Mrs. James Higgins, Richard Higgins, John Knox, Mr. and Mrs. Thomas Lawrence, Mr. and Mrs. Charles Preston and Mr. and Mrs. John Preston.

BENSON:
Carlo Di Mezza.

BLUE MT. LAKE:
Ernest Blanchard, John Kathan.

HOPE:
Mr. and Mrs. Watson Arnold, Wm. Baird, Mr. and Mrs. Ed Call, Harry Craig, Cy Dunham, Donald Wadsworth.

INDIAN LAKE:

Mrs. Katherine Earley, Mrs. Elizabeth Alexander, Mr. and Mrs. Ralph Bonesteel, Benjamin Brooks, Edwin Galusha, Beecher Houghton, Mr. and Mrs. Allie Hunt, Ernest Hutchins, Nat Locke, Mrs. Laura Sprung.

INLET:

K. L. Harwood, Mr. and Mrs. Riley Johnston, Mrs. Laura Bird.

LAKE PLEASANT:

Edward Brooks, Eugene Brooks, Mrs. Nora Brooks, John F. Buyce, Mr. and Mrs. Milton Buyce, Mr. and Mrs. Burr Call, Douglas Call, Mrs. Laura Campbell, L. H. Chequer, Mr. and Mrs. Sanford Courtney, Mrs. Carl Earley, Mr. and Mrs. Clyde Elliott, Mr. and Mrs. Harry Gallup, Mr. and Mrs. Glenn Harrison, Mrs. Eva Higgins, Mrs. Cora Kennell, Mrs. Elizabeth Lawrence, Mr. and Mrs. James Lawrence, Pants Lawrence, Mrs. Goldie Morrison, Mrs. Gordon Morris, Mrs. Charles Nesbit, Lewis Nichols, Mrs. Edward O'Mara, Mrs. Nora Osborne, Robert Osborne, Mr. and Mrs. Wm. Osborne, Mr. and Mrs. John O'Connell, Halsey Page, Selah Page, Thomas Parslow, Ashley Perkins, Gordon Purdy, Col. Van Ness Philip, Mrs. Ida Sturges, Kenneth Sturges, David Shuttleworth, Mrs. Sarah Collie Smith, Charles Wickes, Mr. and Mrs. George Van Zandt, Mrs. Helen York.

LONG LAKE:

Mr. and Mrs. Arthur Parker, Mrs. Ethel Houghton, Ike Robinson, Mrs. Jessie Stone, Andrew Sullivan, Miss Marion Sullivan, Ed Wilson.

RAQUETTE LAKE:

Miss Clara Bryere, Mrs. Dennis Dillon, Sr.

MOREHOUSE:

Mr. and Mrs. Earl Kreuzer, Henry Hart, Earl Farber, Charles Partello, Lester Partello.

WELLS:
John Heffernan, Mr. and Mrs. Hiram Craig, Chris Doak, John Hosley, Lucien Wager, Wallace Wager.

Miss Marion Banker, Gloversville, N.Y.; Mrs. Eva Meyrowitz, Rochester; John Higgins, Daytona Beach, Fla.; John Conover, Amsterdam.

* * * * *

There have been changes in Hamilton County. Many of those quoted herein have passed into the history they helped retell.

Despite this, the text remains unchanged: The writing retains its original flavor. The book continues a backward look at a significant segment of Hamilton County from the vantage point of 1961. We believe the reader will prefer it this way.

TALES
FROM AN
ADIRONDACK COUNTY

LAND OF ENCHANTMENT

MANY MILLIONS of years ago, while the dark, lashing waters of the sea still covered the surface of the restless earth, a freedom-loving land sought to escape its watery chains. Like a waking giant, it began with vigorous determination and ponderous power to thrust violently upward until huge sharp mountains of rock stood out against the deep blue of the sun-filled sky.

Then, as though jealous of promontories that would reach so brazenly toward the stars, the great continental ice cap moved vengefully southward. The summits of the mountains crumbled in its path. Huge rock masses tumbled into fantastic valleys. Abysmal holes were gouged on every side. Finally, as the gigantic glacier withdrew, it left a rocky, tormented countryside in its wake.

Now the fierce ruthlessness of nature gave way to benevolent mood. Rains came over the years to chasten the harshness of the landscape. The starkly gaping holes in the earth were filled with crystal-clear water. Soft green foliage came to clothe the naked, rock-hewn slopes. And sparkling streams from the purest of springs coursed through the welcoming woodlands.

A newly beneficent nature, as though remorseful for the erstwhile havoc it had wrought on the once stricken countryside, added health-giving atmosphere, filled the lakes and streams with food fish, caused tempting game to roam through the cool shaded forests. And, in a final burst of effulgence, a haunting, mystical kind of beauty was bestowed.

The way was prepared for human kind.

It was left to the native Indians to discover the enchanted region and give it name. It was left to man through the years to respond to its lure, to yield to its irresistible charm. For there is a kinship in the heart of man with the heartland of the mountains. And the number is legion whom the Adirondacks continue to hold within their overpowering spell.

The nineteenth century had not yet begun when the first brave pioneers came to seek their fortune in the mountains. In their ears rang the abundant assurances of the sellers of land. In their hearts, as they viewed the mountains' splendour, rose even greater promise.

Capricious, beguiling nature smiled down with satisfaction. Kindly warm spring days gave way to summer's grandeur. Then, its deception complete, deluding nature followed with the longest period of frigid climate, the most brutal of winters the settlers had ever known.

Unending hardship became the lot of these resolute mountain people. Continuous sacrifice became their fate. While the nation around them developed and distant neighbors acquired new prosperity and wealth, the mountain people remained eternal pioneers. No commerce came to rumple their untrammeled wilderness. Theirs remained a community apart. Of grave necessity, they developed a culture of their own.

The occasional sportsman moved ponderously up the rutted mountain roads to find adventure in their midst. Each called the mountains and the mountain lakes the most beautiful he had ever known. Then, his respite ended, he moved southward toward the cities he knew as home. The hardy mountain-dwellers remained.

Legends began to weave their way about the countryside, cloaking the awesome, impressive mountains with even greater mystery than nature itself had proffered. They first found birth around the lonely campfire of the hunter, deep in the shadow of some lofty prominence, with the obscure engulfing woodland darkness all around. Later, as the small mountain communities slowly grew, the stories were repeated at the fireplaces of the few small mountain inns, where the Adirondack guides were wont to gather, or on long winter evenings around the pot-bellied stove at the little village store.

The first story-tellers were the Indians. Living close to the land, observing its vagaries, their legends sought to explain the characteristics of the nature they saw. Pronounced earnestly and stolidly against the impressive silence of the woodland, their fantastic myths had always the tantalizing quality of the bare basis of eternal truth.

The settlers, more particularly the famed Adirondack guides, perpetuated the tradition. Their stories were of local happenings and of local people. They told of hunting exploits, of unsuspectedly wily animals, and uncommonly gifted hunting dogs. And when the small communities failed to yield sufficient fare for a full evening's entertainment around the glowing embers, they were prone to mingle good-natured whimsy with hard-kerneled fact. Out of these stories, the famous tall tales of the Adirondacks were early born and continued to grow.

It has often been repeated that truth is stranger than fiction. And in remote mountain areas, where men live as one with nature, the adage is doubly true. Yet, here in the mountain fastness, fact and fable remain intertwined and intermingled, each complementing the other, each adding to the store of unforgettable lore.

These are the legends, and the people who made them legend, of the beautiful Adirondacks of Hamilton County and neighboring communities. These are the stories that explain, more than fact alone, how a people lived and why the Central Adirondacks wear an aura of unmistakable enchantment, why they are truly a place apart.

THE LEGEND OF SACANDAGA LAKE

EARLY in the nineteenth century and before, there lived on the broad sandy beach at the foot of Lake Pleasant an old Mohawk Indian named Captain Gill. With him dwelt his good squaw, Molly, and a papoose, Molly, junior, whom Gill always claimed was not his own. Around his rawhide tent lay the distant acreage of the earliest of Lake Pleasant's settlers. The year 1805 had not yet begun.

Would-be hunters from the cities to the southward early came upon the venerable Captain Gill. Often-times, he would be their guide.

In the long evenings, when the woodland supper of fresh fish and newly-dressed venison had been consumed and the stars shone brightly overhead, Captain Gill would narrate his age-old legends. Perhaps, he would tell the story of Sacandaga Lake.

Many years ago, he would tell, a long-forgotten Indian tribe lived in the region and lighted its council fires on the hilltop where later the well-remembered Hamilton Inn was to stand.

One winter was especially severe, bitter cold with little snow. The herbage was killed at its roots. The deer and moose wandered to the more hospitable foothills near the Mohawk Valley, where the Indian hunters dared not follow. The fishing, too, failed. Whole families perished. Surrounded by hostile tribes, it was impossible for the Indians to migrate briefly to a new hunting ground nearby.

At a council fire one evening in early spring, the young and enterprising earnestly and urgently proposed a secret migration to the west of Lake Ontario, where wild rice, samples of which had been brought by a runner from a distant nation, would support them in their perilous pilgrimage along the shores.

The old men of the tribe were indignant at such talk of

leaving their homeland. They doubted the existence of the garden regions, the chief said. The famine was a scourge which the Master of Life inflicted on his people for their crimes. Endured with constancy, it would pass away. Flee from it and punishment would follow. Besides, spring had come and soon the land would start producing food again.

Maddened with rage, a hot-blooded young warrior sprang to his feet.

"Let them die!" he shrieked. "Let them die for the crimes they confess!" With their death would come more food for the children. The aged would only impede a major journey in any case. With a ferocious whoop, the young barbarian buried his tomahawk in the head of the old man nearest him. Other young warriors followed his lead and seven old tribesmen were instantly killed.

In the horrified silence that followed, realization of the magnitude of the crime engulfed them. Deepest reverence for the aged was an old Indian tradition.

It was decided to sanctify the deed, as best they could, by offering up the bodies of the slaughtered to the Master of Life. They would decapitate the victims and burn their bodies, sinking the heads together into Sacandaga Lake.

The young chief who had suggested the bloody scene led the procession of canoes, one head being carried in each. At a designated spot, the heads were passed to him to be tied together by their scalp-locks and sunk with a huge stone to the bottom of Sacandaga Lake.

But the vengeance of the Master of Life overtook the young leader. No sooner had he received the last head, than his canoe began to sink. His feet became entangled in the hideous chain he had fashioned and, before his horror-stricken companions could come to his rescue, the young red-skin was dragged shrieking to the bottom. The others paddled hastily to shore.

The following day, a few gory bubbles rose to the surface. The second day, the sullen blot remained. The third day, it took a greener hue and strands of black marbled its surface. On the fourth day, these marks began to tremble.

By the sixth day, a monstrous head floated on the water, its huge eyes watching the guilty young Indians constantly. On the morning of the seventh day, a pair of broad wings, ribbed like those of a bat, with claws appended to each tendon, had grown from the head. As the young warriors watched, the wings flapped harshly once or twice upon the waves, and the head rose slowly from the lake.

The Indian parricides fled in panic, but the terrible Flying Head followed. Wherever they went, whatever they did, the monster pursued, glaring at them constantly.

What was the outcome? Some say the Master of Life kept them forever young so that their suffering might endure. Others insist that the Flying Head still pursues them over the prairies of the West. Still others hold that the glances of the Flying Head turned them gradually to stone and that their forms, though altered by the wearing of the rains, can still be recognized in those upright rocks that stand like human figures along the shores of some of the neighboring lakes.

There were those Indians who declared that the monstrous Flying Head had appeared to them more than once over the lake that gave it birth. Certain it is that the Flying Head always returns to this part of the country about the times of the Equinox. Some say you can always hear the flapping of its giant wings whenever a thunderstorm brews.

THE LEGEND OF PISECO

AN UNEARTHLY STILLNESS would grip the mountain fastness. Only the lonely hoot of a distant owl would punctuate the overwhelming quiet of the night. The bright-red embers of the campfire would rise occasionally to fluttering flame, in a vain attempt to pierce the surrounding tree-shaded blackness. Weary muscles would tell that it was time for the city sportsman of the early 1800's to bed down for the night.

Then it was that the sonorous voice of Captain Gill, their Mohawk Indian guide, might be heard in the legend of the Otne-Yar-Heh or Stone Giants. Quietly, his listeners would be told of those strange forms resembling men that stand, as though carved from solid rock, like sentinels along the shores of the Southern Adirondacks' numerous lakes. They were first discovered at Piseco Lake.

It seems, Captain Gill would relate, that a band of strange Indians had appeared in the area and had encamped on the sand beach of Piseco, about a gunshot from the cove where the Oxbow inlet enters the lake.

They were discovered and attacked by a war-party of Iroquois on its way to strike a blow against the Abenakis. Mistaking them for Hurons, the Iroquois killed or gravely wounded these strange Indians. Only too late did they discover their error. Unwilling to carry the wounded back to their villages, the Iroquois determined to leave them to their fate.

The vengeance of the Master of Life was felt when not one of these Iroquois warriors ever returned to his home.

Meanwhile, the bleeding band crawled to the water's edge to quench their overpowering thirst in Piseco's waters. They writhed in agony on the shore, the sand particles mingling with their gore and congealing almost like solid rock around them. As they drank of the lake waters, their bodies grew into frightful hulks until they breathed their last.

[7]

Winter came and preserved these crusted remains from decay. And, when the snows subsided, each stark, grim corpse had grown to massive size, while the waves of the lake, in washing its shells and pebbles over them, appeared to have turned them into solid masses of stone.

Now came the carnivorous grizzly bears. Beginning with the feet, they ate their way into the gigantic molds, only to find themselves trapped. Yet they found that the flinty casing yielded to their every motion and that, if they stood erect, they could walk as before.

Immediately, the giant band went over mountain and lake to the homes of the Iroquois. A long series of battles ensued, with no weapons of any kind having the least effect on the stone giants.

At length, it was decided that the chief men of the Five Nations should meet at Onondaga in order to take up common defense against this formidable enemy. This is how the famous league of five nations was formed.

The Master of Life looked so benignantly upon the councils of this band of brothers that he sent his lightning among the Otne-Yar-Heh, driving the giants back into the mountains. He further ringed the area with thunderbolts, so that no game could enter, and the stone giants perished.

Their only traces are the giant rock forms scattered among these highlands. And, since that time, no grizzly bear has been seen within a hundred miles of these lakes.

GRIEF COMES TO THE ISDELLS

THE NATIVE INDIANS continued to roam the Southern Adirondacks for many years after the first white settlers began to push their way up the tortured mountain trails. Encounters with these inscrutable and frequently fearsome neighbors formed the basis of tales that sometimes chilled the hearts of the pioneer's diligent wife and unsuspecting children.

So it was in the spring of 1801, when young David Isdell came to purchase land along the clear-flowing waters of the Sacandaga River in the present Town of Hope. Here the stolid Scotsman painstakingly built his solitary, indomitable dwelling, the first within the confines of the present Hamilton County to be constructed of native stone. Mindful of his family's safety, he fashioned, too, an underground passage that led from a point near the south fireplace out past the old heavy-timbered barn and about a quarter of a mile beyond to a huge rock hidden in a thick evergreen grove.

The house was sturdily built. Only in recent years has the old stone chimney that stood for years, a landmark beside the highway, finally toppled to the ground. Protection from the Indians was the builder's goal.

The Isdells had ample reason to remember the Indians of the region.

One bright carefree morning, when the summer sun shone warmly down on the embowering pines and glistened happily on the rippling waters of the nearby Sacandaga, Catherine and Ruth Isdell set out for a day of berrying. With them went their romping six-year-old, fair-haired sister, Mary.

Throughout the morning, the berrying continued. Then lunch was spread on a grassy bank not far from the river's edge.

Mindful that their work was but half concluded, the two elder sisters soon renewed their efforts, determined to bring home a worthy reward. But the young Mary was weary after her pleasant meal. Slowly, she roamed away in search of a moss-covered log on which to lay her head and nap.

She had wandered for some time. Suddenly, from behind a clump of brush, the tall bronzed figure of an Indian appeared. The tired Mary made no resistance as she was picked up in his brawny arms and was restfully carried away.

At length, a rising mountain breeze whispered softly in the treetops and the tall sentinel pines cast long cool shadows on the rock-filled soil. Well-filled pails indicated that the day's work had been well done. Catherine and Ruth Isdell decided to return to their home.

For the first time, they missed their little sister. Several times they called her name. Only the silent woodland answered. Then, confident that the six-year-old had preceded them, they set out slowly for the familiar stone house.

Consternation was general when it was learned that young Mary had not returned. With mounting fear, a thorough search of the woods was begun. At length, distant neighbors were recruited. Throughout the night and for many days thereafter, the quest continued. No trace of the lost Mary remained.

A grief-stricken family faced the stark realization that their daughter might never return. Still, an occasional glimmer of hope persisted. But, finally, a full year passed and hope of ever finding the little girl had vanished.

One day, a bent old man came to the Isdell house. He walked with a shuffling gait and with the aid of a cane. His whole being bore an air of mystery. No one ever knew his name.

The strange old visitor remained for several days. It was impossible for him not to be aware of an all-encompassing depression that filled the household. Soon he learned about the lost child.

He was silent for a time as he shuffled to the fireplace and stood looking at the burning logs. Then, with a whimsical smile, he turned.

"I have the gift of prophecy," he said. "I foresee news of your daughter. I don't know when, but it will come before long."

No one spoke. Wordlessly, the old man shuffled out the doorway, never to return.

The Isdells waited hopefully for the predicted message. None came.

One day, a tow-headed boy in his teens came hastening anxiously to their door. His clothes were tattered, his face scratched and torn. Rest and food were his needs.

Hungrily, the boy wolfed down the wholesome home-baked bread, delicious venison stew, and cool, refreshing milk that the kindly Mrs. Isdell provided. During the infrequent pauses, his story was told.

He had escaped from the Indians far to the northward and was making his way homeward. Nor was he the only white child among them. Scant days before his departure, a young, light-haired girl had died in the Indian encampment and had been buried in the woods nearby.

Sadly, Mrs. Isdell raised tear-filled eyes to her husband. The David Isdells realized that they would never see their beloved little daughter again.

THE GRAVE OF LORING PECK

EACH YEAR, as regular as clockwork, representatives of the American Legion Post of Speculator make a Memorial Day pilgrimage deep into the woods on Lake Pleasant's southern side. At the end of a long and twisted trail, cluttered at intervals by fallen tree trunks, half-hidden at times by encroaching brush, they ascend a tree-covered knoll. Here, in the deep shadows of the woodland, is a small family burial plot, surrounded by a stone fence with an opening at the side. Beside one of the three time-worn, weather-beaten tombstones, an American flag is placed. Then, their homage performed, they return to the village, leaving the sleeping dead to the profound silence of the brooding mountain land.

The same walk through the woods is a favorite with summer residents and summer visitors. Few know the significance of the graveyard, yet the strange feeling of somehow having walked backward in history a hundred and fifty years is theirs. The heritage of the past is unmistakably experienced as quietly they read the well-preserved legends on the stones:

"Col. Loring Peck, a patriot of the Revolution, died July 29, 1833 in his 90th year."

"Jane, his wife, died June 20, 1825 in her 71st year."

"Loring Peck, Jr., died May 5, 1861 in his 80th year."

Lake Pleasant men of the early days liked to boast of their new neighbor, Col. Loring Peck, and his illustrious sons.

Descendant of a family that had come to New England in 1638, Loring Peck was a zealous patriot. The son of Jonathan and Hannah Wood Peck of Bristol, Rhode Island, he had entered military service at an early age. By January, 1775, he had become a captain. During the War of the Revolution, Peck was promoted to major. In 1794, as commander of the Senior Class Regiment of Rhode Island troops of Newport and Bristol Counties, he became lieutenant colonel, a rank he held throughout his continuous service through 1797. He was also a member of the Rhode Island Legislature for many years.

In May, 1798, Col. Loring Peck with Jane Burke, his second wife, and their family, left Bristol, R.I. to settle in Amenia, Dutchess County, N.Y. In 1811, they removed to the Town of Lake Pleasant. Here Loring and his newly-married oldest son, William Burke Peck, bought adjoining farmlands of Amos and Ebenezer Green to the southeast of Lake Pleasant toward the base of Speculator Mountain in Township One.

Diligently, they cleared the land and built their houses, fastening together the rough-hewn boards with carefully hand-wrought nails. Painstakingly, they planted orchards and tilled the rocky soil. Back-breaking work was performed to make roads past their properties. At length, they were rewarded by thrifty mountain farms, with cattle, sheep, horses and hogs.

The Pecks were ever conscious of the proud military tradition of their family. When the continuing turmoil with Great Britain erupted violently into the War of 1812, the sons of Loring Peck responded. Educated for the professions, Dr. George Peck was both a physician and surgeon and surveyor and engineer. Without hesitation, he volunteered as surgeon for the duration of the war. Strong, energetic and decisive, William Burke Peck held an army commission and saw service on the frontier or Canadian line.

In civil affairs, the Pecks were equally qualified to serve their fellows. William Burke Peck became the first town clerk when the Town of Lake Pleasant was established on April 7, 1812.

With the formation of Hamilton County on February 12, 1816, Richard Peck became its first judge and later served as member of the State Assembly. For many years, he and his brother were chosen alternately supervisor or town clerk of their town.

As the years moved onward and the clouds of Civil War darkened the land, the sons of Richard Peck, then a resident of Wells, responded once more to their military calling. Charles H. and Walter B. Peck volunteered early for service. In 1863, William B. Peck resigned the office he had held for many years as county clerk and entered the army, stating in a letter to a relative that he was anxious "to hand down to my children the inheritance so nobly bequeathed to them by their honored grandsire." He was killed in the Battle of the Wilderness on May 8, 1864.

Time has long since changed the landscape where once the Peck family lived. The forest has reclaimed the well-kept fields. The lowing of the cattle is heard no more. Farm buildings have disintegrated with decay and travelled roads, once carved with such back-breaking toil from the wilderness, are scarcely to be found.

Today, the half-hidden woodland way to the original Peck lands leads through a leafy glade edged on either side by a rough fence of native stone, diligently piled by an ancient hand. The path travels an old, abandoned roadway that led long ago to Guide Board Hill on the old military road above Gilman Lake on the way between Speculator and Wells.

Across a small stream and up a gentle slope, one suddenly comes to an open area in the forest. As one walks onward through the deep grass, an old foundation is seen, and a forlorn and thirsty well, dry to its fullest depth. In the distance stands green and imperious Speculator Mountain, massive, inscrutable, proud. Here, beyond the bounds of modern civilization, rest the inconclusive remains of the house of Col. Loring Peck. The desolate graveyard lies beyond.

Here the observer stands in quiet reverence amid the deep silence of the forest, conscious of nature's loveliness all around. Somewhere nearby, an unseen bird sings tentatively. And perhaps, for one brief moment, in the heart of the onlooker, the true glory of a free America lives once more.

THE LAUDABLE FORESIGHT
OF ZADOK BASS

ZADOK BASS, JR. came to the Town of Arietta from his native Hope to buy land of Andrew K. Morehouse on April 18, 1835. With him, he brought a variety of native talents and a willingness to perform any number of trades to help carve a meager living from the reluctant wilderness. If his goal was modest, it was difficult to achieve in the mountains of his day.

Among his many achievements, Zadok became the original coffin-maker of the community and lost no opportunity to practice the scanty trade that supplemented his farming efforts.

About the year 1860, a young feminine invalid was brought by her parents to Zadok's native Rudeston in an attempt to have her flagging health restored. But, as time elapsed, the girl's condition failed to show improvement and fears were expressed that her recovery would never come to pass.

It was then that the energetic Zadok Bass arrived on the scene, carrying a stick he always used to measure a corpse for its coffin. Without hesitation, he took the dimensions of the languishing lass. The community gasped when it was learned that the coffin was ready. Zadok had it virtually on the doorstep as the ailing patient breathed her last.

NICK STONER AND THE INDIANS

SOME YEARS before the old military road was built, two huge logs were placed side by side over the outlet of Lake Pleasant for hiking men to cross. The legend is told that the professional hunter, Nick Stoner, once started across the rude bridge from the south just as an implacable, surly Indian, bearing his pelts to market, started to cross from the north.

The details of what transpired when these two immovable objects met at midpoint are not recorded. But when the melee ended, Nick Stoner is said to have been walking southward, well weighted with marketable pelts.

The story is not surprising. Nick Stoner's deep abiding hatred for Indians was well-known. Not without reason!

While Nick was away in military service during the American Revolution, his father, Henry Stoner, had been surprised while hoeing corn on his farm in the Town of Mayfield. He had been summarily scalped and killed by two Indians in the British service.

Nick got his revenge after the war. Striding into the barroom of De Fonclaiere's Johnstown inn, the hunter heard an Indian bragging that a deep-cut notch on the handle of his scalping knife represented the scalp he had taken of "old Stoner." Springing to the fireplace, Nick seized a red-hot andiron and flung it at the Indian's head. Nick was jailed but was soon released when the vehement protests of the populace showed overwhelmingly that, in their opinion, only justice had been done. The redman is believed to have died while being borne toward Canada. Let the Indian who ever crossed Nick Stoner's trail beware!

Stoner knew the Southern Adirondacks well. It was he who guided the surveyors of the road from Johnstown to Oxbow Lake. Once, when the party was out of food, he crossed the wilderness to the Denny house on Sacandaga Lake and gained sustenance for the party to go on. Again, he showed that the mountains can provide unsuspected delicacies at the hands of a skillful guide. One day, he captured a large turtle on the shore of Piseco Lake. From its one hundred and seventy-two eggs, he made eggnog, cooling the drink with ice he had discovered in a crevice between some rocks the previous day. The turtle's meat then provided a tasty repast.

One of Stoner's last encounters with the Indians occurred at Lake Pleasant in the year 1822. Stoner had come to Oxbow Lake to join his friend, Shadrack Dunning, in retrieving traps that Dunning had left in the woods. On their way, Stoner set two traps for beaver, another for otter, and killed and skinned a moose. The two men sank the moose hide in the water to remove the hair, and hung two muskrat skins on a nearby tree. That representing a day's work, they stayed overnight in a deserted hunter's camp that appeared to have been recently occupied.

The next day, they found that their otter trap had disappeared and Indian tracks were discovered at the place it had been set. The other two traps were intact, except that, in one, a beaver had been caught and had escaped by gnawing off its own leg. The third trap contained an otter.

Having recovered Dunning's traps and spent several days in hunting, they started their return trip. One of their original traps was found, robbed of its game, and suspended by its jaws from a nearby stump. Some of their moose-skin had been cut away and the muskrat pelts were gone.

Arriving at the Dunning home on Saturday night, they learned that two Indian trappers had just reached the Lake Pleasant settlement, four miles distant. The two lost no time in getting to George Wright's inn, where they found that the two Indians were encamped in the woods about a hundred yards away.

Darkness prevented their visiting the camp. Stoner was aroused during the night by Wright's nephew waking the inn-keeper to tell him that the Indians' dogs were killing sheep. Stoner and the boy found, in driving the dogs away, that one sheep had already been killed.

The next morning, Stoner visited the Indians, finding one to be Captain Sabael Benedict, the Abenaki Indian who lived on the shores of Indian Lake. Stoner knew and respected Benedict, but became less impressed with his companion, introduced as Francis, who was quaffing rum from a jug. Anticipating fun, George Wright, Lewis Williams, the grocer, and one of the Peck brothers hid behind nearby trees.

Stoner had no trouble in seeing thongs of his own moose-hide tying together several traps, including his own. Grabbing the traps, he started cutting loose his own. Francis tried to prevent him.

"No cut him! No cut him!" the Indian protested.

In anger and disgust, Nick Stoner threw the whole bundle of heavy traps at the Indian, knocking him flat on the ground.

"If trap yours, take him," the Indian murmured lamely as he regained his feet.

Apparently ashamed of his companion, Captain Benedict

tried to show his friendliness by offering Stoner a drink of his rum. Momentarily pacified, the hunter accepted. In a similar show of cordiality, he invited the Indians to the tavern for a drink with him. Both Indians accompanied him, but, at the bar, Francis insolently refused to drink.

Incensed, Stoner smashed the liquor-filled tumbler against his head. The Indian closed for a fight, but shortly found himself pitched bodily out of the barroom door and lying flat on the ground, gravel buried in his head and cheek. Bystanders stopped the fight.

There was a pause to let passions cool. Stoner demanded that Francis either return the stolen furs or pay for them. Together, they went across the inlet to the grocery where Lewis G. Williams dealt principally in ammunition, blankets, rum and staples. Here they found the green beaver-skin that the Indian had sold there the previous afternoon.

Finally, Francis admitted having taken the skin from the trap, but denied having stolen the two muskrat pelts. Instead, he suggested that it was probably the work of five young Indians then hunting in the area.

A compromise was made. Francis paid Stoner an agreed sum. Stoner dictated the receipt to Williams.

The five young accused Indians entered, bearing several marten skins but not one muskrat pelt. One was Lige Ell, a son of Sabael. When told of Francis' accusation, he was highly insulted. At the first opportunity, he advised Francis that if he wanted to live, he would never show himself in that region again. It is believed that the Indian never returned.

LAKE PLEASANT'S HAUNTED HOUSE

THERE WAS the dream some day of large and comfortable houses, as the early settlers of Lake Pleasant struggled to tame the wilderness and hew their rough log cabins. Yet this, in the year 1815, was not to be. The most impossible thing they could have imagined was that a manor house would be placed among them in their young mountain town.

And then the impossible happened!

Philip Rhinelander, Jr., of the prominent and wealthy family of New York City merchants, owners of Township Nine, was twenty-seven years old when he came, with slaves and servants, to develop his family's holdings. The 300-acre estate he cleared and built overlooking picturesque little Elm Lake was elegant by any criterion. By the rough standards of the young mountain settlement of Lake Pleasant, it was magnificent.

A center hall with dark mahogany staircase ran the length of the mansion. Off the hallway were large rooms, two with huge fireplaces. In the kitchen was a vast elevated oven, constructed of clay bricks made on the premises across the water from the Elm Lake Place. Handmade nails, fashioned on the estate, were also used in the construction. Master bedrooms of significant dimension opened off the large center hall on the second floor.

The house was lavishly furnished with mahogany furniture and beautiful paintings. A melodeon and marble-top table long after remained in the ownership of Meade Sturges.

At the front of the house was a cut-stone terrace. A park stood at the side. Toward the lake, where the lawns sloped gently down, was a massive flower garden. Nearby were vast orchards where apples, plums and pears were grown, and a vineyard to furnish grapes to the family larder.

At the rear were the outhouses for the Negro servants, with a private cemetery where they might bury their dead. Further back stood the stables and carriage houses. And there was a creamery, with wooden racks for holding milk containers, and barns for storing hay.

A pretty stream flowed down the hillside and through the well-kept grounds. Here it was said the servants performed their family washings.

Far down at the outlet of Lake Pleasant, near the present bridge on the main highway where the still waters cascade to become the roaring Sacandaga, Rhinelander built a grist and sawmill.

There were 100 acres of land in crops at Elm Lake. Cattle, horses and sheep were sent from New York to graze in the ample fields. And there were oxen and sleighs with wooden runners.

The mountains looked jealously down.

Philip Rhinelander, Jr. worked alike to develop his property and to help forward the affairs of the new community of which he was a part. If the public life of the landed proprietor was unquestioned, the fanciful legends that for years surrounded life on his Elm Lake estate now began to arise.

He had married Mary Colden Hoffman, daughter of the Hon. Josiah C. Hoffman and his wife, Mary Colden, described as a singularly beautiful girl. To them in 1815 was born Philip R. Rhinelander, who later lived in Vienna and died a bachelor there on August 12, 1839. A daughter, Mary Colden Rhinelander, was born while the family lived in the mountains, on April 7, 1818.

The conveniences and luxuries of the Elm Lake home were only the outward expression of the deep love that Philip Rhinelander, Jr. held for his young wife. But love was said to have been coupled with almost equally intense jealousy. People said the young Mrs. Rhinelander was kept virtually a prisoner in her lovely home.

From time to time, she would write letters to friends back home in New York City, it was said, giving them to her hus-

band to mail. Once out of her sight, the letters were torn to
bits. Lonely and heartsick, she found herself cut off from the
outside world.

At times, she tried to get messages to people in other ways.
Once, a lone pack peddler came to the door of the Rhinelander
Mansion and talked to Mrs. Rhinelander, the stories relate. He
was later found dead in a spring on the Elm Lake Estate
grounds.

Another story told of a washwoman, servant of the household, who was befriended by Mrs. Rhinelander. Later, she was
found dead.

Rumors increased among the townspeople, most of whom
had never stepped inside the awesome mansion at Elm Lake.
Time and the retelling only served to embellish them further. If
they were misconception, they were none-the-less intriguing.
The mansion at Elm Lake was irrevocably enriched with a
garment of apocryphal lore.

In the late summer of 1818, Mary Colden Rhinelander became ill. On September 7th, she died. Again rumors circulated
among the townsfolk that slow poisoning had been the cause.

Unwilling, perhaps, to be separated even in death from the
wife he so dearly loved, Philip Rhinelander had a vault built
near his mansion in which his wife's body was kept until
spring, when it was taken to New York City for burial.

Philip Rhinelander remained on his estate until the summer
of 1823. Then, shortly after being elected supervisor of the
Town of Lake Pleasant for the second time, he was seized with
paralysis and left for New York City, never to return. Seven
years later, he was dead.

For about four years, the property was occupied by the
Englishman, Thomas Wayne. Later, the house was kept partly
boarded up and a caretaker was employed. Gradually, it became known that the house was haunted. Only the hard-headed
believed otherwise. The evidence was too wide-spread and too
strong.

Cows were still kept on the estate for some years and the

caretaker caused haying to be done. At first, the men would remain overnight, sleeping in the lonely rooms of the deserted mansion, but the room formerly occupied by the deceased Mrs. Rhinelander soon became roundly shunned. In the inky stillness of the night, a woman could be seen coming toward the bed, with plainly audible grief-stricken sobs resounding. When the men reached out to touch her, the apparition was gone. On another occasion, when one of the local workmen slept in the same room, he was disturbed by the sound of rustling skirts, voices raised in animated conversation, and he could "hear her combing her hair."

Soon sleep in other rooms became equally disturbed. At midnight, a man could be heard mounting the staircase, the hard leather heels of his riding boots clicking sharply on each progressive stair. Sometimes, the ghost seemed to be turning handsprings. Or again, the very bed-clothes would be pulled from the would-be sleeper, and there were often the unearthly sounds of something being dragged downstairs.

Once, a ghostlike figure was both seen and heard making its way through the hallways and into the drawing room, where it seemed to disappear into the boarded fireplace. The men tore the boards from the fireplace but nothing was found. At another time, a pumpkin came hurtling down the long center hall, striking against the far wall.

After a time, Isaac Page was employed as caretaker of the estate. The day their son died, Mrs. Page went to their home, leaving one of her daughters behind to complete the chores. The young girl milked the cows, strained the milk, and put it in containers on the shelf. Suddenly, the candles used for lighting the room were tossed into the air by an invisible force. Armed with stove pokers, the girl and her father searched the house from top to bottom but found nothing at all.

In view of this strange occurrence, several women from the town agreed to stay with the Page girl the following night. It was a warm evening and the women walked outside in the park. Suddenly, there was a whirlwind in the leaves. Madly, it came swirling around the house and careened crazily off toward Mrs. Rhinelander's empty vault. One of the women fainted.

Even the men working in the fields were not spared. The woman who used to wash her clothes in the stream could frequently be seen, it seemed, and it was said that she haunted the grounds of the estate. The farmers were always pleased to leave the place to its ghosts each night before dusk had fallen.

The Rhinelander family seldom if ever came near the place. Most of the furniture was eventually auctioned off to pay delinquent taxes. Some of it still remains in local homes.

One night, around the year 1874, the abandoned mansion, a mere memory of its former elegance, caught fire and was burned to the ground. The sheds were left to decay. The International Paper Company now owns and lumbers the land.

The forests have long since reclaimed the grounds and the road to the site of the former Rhinelander estate is hazardous to motor travel. Surrounded by dense forest, the ruins of the once magnificent mansion exist close to the side of the unfrequented dirt road, difficult to find.

As for the ghosts? Perhaps even yet, on quiet, lonely nights when the soft pale moon is half-hidden at intervals by shapeless scurrying clouds, their restless, eerie forms return at midnight to haunt the impassive, secluded spot where once a lordly manor was their home.

A LIFETIME IN THE WOODS

ONE OF the most famous professional hunters at mid-century and beyond was Alvah Dunning. Known throughout the central and Southern Adirondacks for his woodsmanship and his rustic mode of living, the noted woodsman inspired stories that are legion. Some, like that of his ancestry, are not entirely founded in fact.

The legend has grown that Alvah was a son of "Scout" Dunning, who served under Sir William Johnson in pre-Revolutionary War years. The authenticated history of the Dunning family does not substantiate the story. There is obvious confusion between the Dunning and Dunham families, both of which lived at Lake Pleasant in its earliest years. If immortalization of the huntsman is its purpose, the colorful life of Alvah Dunning is in itself sufficient to place him high on the list of favored stories of Adirondack men.

The Dunning family was native to Connecticut, where Alvah's grandfather, Amos Dunning, was born around 1763. By 1810, the family had moved to Lake Pleasant.

Shadrack Dunning, father of Alvah, was born in South Parish, Woodbury, Conn., some fifteen years after the death of Sir William Johnson and after the conclusion of the Revolutionary War. He came with his family to Lake Pleasant and about 1809 married Mary Nichols. After her death, he married, as his second wife, Dorcas Greene, around 1815. Their first child, Alvah Greene Dunning, was born June 14, 1816.

An adept hunter and trapper, Shadrack Dunning lived near Oxbow Lake. Young Alvah began to hunt and trap with his father when he was six years old. He is said to have killed his first moose at the age of eleven and to have guided his first party at the age of twelve.

As a young man, Alvah moved with his family to Piseco Lake, where his father ran a sawmill for a time. While there, he killed 102 panthers in eight years. The biggest catch of fish was made in 1833, when he pulled 96 pounds of salmon trout from Piseco in two hours. The largest salmon trout on record, weighing 27½ pounds, was caught by Alvah's hook. It was said that the number of beasts brought down by his gun, exclusive of the smaller game like foxes, mink, otter, and birds, would reach into the thousands.

Alvah Dunning was essentially a primitive man who thoroughly knew the woods, the habits of birds and animals, and who lived by his rod and gun. He could entice the mink from its hole by imitating its call and lure frightened deer to the water's edge by deceptive bleatings and splashings with his hands. The Indians called him "Snake Eyes" because he could out-hunt and out-trap them at all times.

Early in his career, Alvah showed his interest in woodland living by packing his knapsack with scant provisions and, with gun, dog and traps, going deep into the forest by way of the old Military Trail. Across the Miami River, he built his crude bark shanty and set his traps. So engrossed did he become in his project and simple mode of living that he stayed all season, building a canoe of white birch, and sealing it with spruce roots and pine pitch. He took more skins to his credit than any other hunter, while adding substantially to his season's earnings by the bounty paid on wolves.

Alvah had a particular hatred for wolves because of their vicious killing of deer. He may be given credit for helping to eradicate them from the Adirondacks.

Perhaps it was his love for the woods that interfered with Alvah's domestic life. In any case, the hunter felt obliged to leave Piseco Lake in 1860, when he outraged public feeling by beating his wife, who had been unfaithful to him. His marriage had lasted two years. Immediately, he went deeper into the Adirondack heartland.

Making his way first to Indian Lake, he spent some time with the Abenaki Indian, Sabael Benedict. Leaving Sabael, he trapped up the Cedar River and took a trail from what is known as the George McCane place to Blue Mountain Lake. Here he was hired as a guide by Edward Zane Carroll Judson, who, as Ned Buntline, popularized the dime novel. The unlikely partnership was not of long standing, for the two had very different views about the killing of game. Theirs was a famous feud.

Alvah saw no logical justification for game laws. He was sparing of fish and forest animals. He killed a deer or caught a trout only when he needed food. It was sinful to kill wastefully, he had decided, and he destroyed less game than many who championed the conservation laws.

After his unfavorable domestic experience at Piseco, Alvah Dunning's life was a long retreat from civilization. He heartily disliked women, calling them "pizen." He rebelled against city people, whom he called "them city dudes with velvet suits and pop guns that can't hit a deer when they see it and don't want it if they do hit it." He rebelled against property laws that would not recognize his squatter's rights. He rebelled against newfangled inventions. His home was among the trees and he knew every tree, every flower, and every forest animal.

Dunning claimed to have killed the last moose in the Adirondacks in 1862.

As time went on, Dunning wandered from one secluded spot to another, seeking solitude in the mountains, a feat that was becoming increasingly difficult with the arrival of ever greater numbers of vacationers and would-be hunters. For years, he lived on Long Lake. Later, he built a camp on Osprey Island in Raquette Lake, where he lived his simple, lonely life. Around him, on the lake shores, were the luxurious cottages of the rich. But, though he mingled with these people, Alvah remained uncontaminated by the habits of civilization.

They were funny people, these city folks. Why, one had even tried to tell Alvah, as they walked through the woods, that the earth was round and turning over and over. It was ridiculous, of course, but when Alvah laughed about this fellow to other visitors to the mountains, they didn't ever quite seem to get the same humor from the story. Alvah knew better than to believe that the earth was round and he had simple, effective proof. He would simply fill a cup with water and turn it upside down.

"Ain't that what wud happen to yer lakes and rivers if yeh turned 'em upside down? I ain't believin' no such tommyrot as that!"

And he never did.

One day, while hauling a large trout into his boat, to his

horror and sorrow, the old guide's silver watch dropped over-board and sank irretrievably into the waters of Raquette Lake. Alvah grieved pitifully. Thereupon, a summer resident, Dr. A. P. Gerster, whose hobby was etching, conceived the idea of etching a plate from a photograph of the old man taken by Stoddard. Two were placed on sale for five dollars at the church fair held at St. Hubert's of Raquette Lake. They were purchased at once. Later, in New York City, an additional eighteen etchings were printed and sold. The total take amounted to one hundred dollars.

With this money, a gold watch was purchased at Benedict's, the proprietor adding, as his own contribution, an elegant gold chain.

At the Christmas celebration at Camp Pine Knot, the gift was handed to Alvah by Will Durant. The old guide toppled over in a dead faint.*

Alvah used the watch for about a year, then to his despair, it was broken. The hermit handed the watch to Will Durant, with the request that he have it repaired. Durant agreed, but pressure of business caused him to forget to return the gold time-piece from New York.

The old guide's well-known cantankerousness immediately came to the fore. Durant had stolen his watch, Alvah declared. As he spoke, he would reach for a long leather string at his belt and pull an alarm clock from his rear pocket. It was his way of attempting to discredit the area's benefactor with Adirondack men.

About the year 1896, Alvah was living in a hut near the west inlet of Raquette Lake. He had remained happily there for about three years when along came a dignified stranger, armed with a briefcase filled with legal-looking documents and a place for Alvah to sign. The very site on which Alvah lived was needed for a railroad station.

* Dr. A. P. Gerster. *Recollections of a New York Surgeon.* New York. Hoeber. 1917.

The old huntsman was stunned. Unbelievingly and almost mechanically, he signed where directed and, watching the intruder disappear in the woodlands, he realized that once more it was time to move on.

"I guess I've lived too long," he murmured mournfully.

Three years later, he bade goodbye to his associates and set out for the Rocky Mountains in search of "a quiet corner out o' reach o' tootin' steamboats and screechin' en-gines." He was back in a year at Raquette Lake, but he was a changed Alvah, bitterly disappointed with the changing world. He travelled more frequently. In his last years, he spent his winters principally with his sister, Mrs. Charles Potter, in Syracuse.

In view of his distaste for modern inventions, the manner of his death proved a crowning irony. In March, 1902, he attended the Sportsmen's Show in New York City. On his return, he spent the night of March 14th at the Dudley House in Utica. The next morning, he was found asphyxiated in his bed. The gas jet had been leaking all night. Alvah had blown out the light.

Some have said that Alvah was the last of his type. It is doubtful, indeed. For something of Alvah Dunning lives in the heart of every sportsman, and for it he is a better man.

RESOURCEFULNESS MARKS
THE WOODSMAN

THE BARBER SATTERLEES from Rhode Island settled early in the Southern Adirondacks, locating north of the present Village of Speculator near Fish Hatchery Brook on the Indian Lake road. Time after time, redmen would be seen skulking in the shadows or moving stolidly along the trail before their cabin door. Apprehensive, the Satterlees removed for a time from the locality. After the close of the War of 1812, they returned.

The Satterlee name was to remain prominent in the Lake Pleasant area for many years. Barber's son, Clark, was to operate the first small inn in the locality that was later to be named Newton's Corners. Clark's son, Toles, was to manage the first store at the four corners nearby.

As a boy, Clark Satterlee early established his reputation as a resourceful hunter.

It was a bright morning in early March of 1822 when sixteen-year-old Clark Satterlee set out with his faithful hunting dog, "Old Sound," to clean and set the troughs in the maple sugar grove in the valley about a half mile away from their house. He would return for breakfast, he told his family.

His parents, Barber and Lucy Satterlee, became concerned when he had not returned by noon. Mindful that he carried no weapon, not even a jackknife, old Barber Satterlee started out in search of the boy. He met his son returning to the house, obviously tired from physical exertion.

Asked where he had been, Clark replied that he had had business to attend to; that he had been killing deer.

"Killing deer?" his father asked incredulously. "How? Gouging out their eyes? You've got nothing to kill a deer with."

Clark told how, in the snowfall of the previous night, he had seen the tracks of four deer in the sugar bush. Anxious for sport, Old Sound had followed their scent and Clark had joined the chase. One of the deer had run into the deep snow under the trees and had become bogged. As Clark came into sight, Old Sound had seized the deer and dragged it into the snow, fully expecting his master to take advantage of the opportunity he was providing.

Unarmed, Clark was momentarily at a loss, until he suddenly saw a large, old, decayed spruce log. As he suspected, it contained a huge, hard, spruce knot. Clark grabbed the knot, charged the deer and, with his primitive weapon, struck the animal in the head and killed it. Relatively the same thing happened with a second deer, and the third.

The fourth deer reached the Kunjamuck River and plunged into a small hole in the ice. Old Sound followed on the ice and, watching his chance, seized the deer by the nose with his teeth, attempting to pull it from the icy waters. With all its might, the deer resisted, placing its forefeet against the ice and holding firm.

Afraid that his dog would be pulled into the water and under the ice, Clark Satterlee ran onto the ice and knocked the deer in the head with his spruce knot. He had killed four deer before noon, and without a gun.

Old Sound was not always as proudly successful in his deer hunting. Some time later, with his master and two other hunters on snowshoes, he came to the large perpendicular stone ledge on the side of Dug Mountain. There he roused a fine three-year-old buck, afterward described by Clark as "the cunningest deer I ever see'd!"

Panic-stricken, the deer began to climb the edge of the ledge. Old Sound was less successful in pursuit. After falling back several times, he followed along the base of the cliff to the opposite side. The deer perched perilously on the ledge, then went down the other side. Old Sound was waiting, and the chase was renewed.

Hurrying to overtake both deer and dog, two of the hunters, less accustomed to snowshoes, fell in the snow. Clark Satterlee came in sight of the deer alone, surprised that he had heard no barking of his dog for some time. There stood the deer in the snow, bolt upright, with its feet gathered under it, and with bristles raised as if to spring. But it remained perfectly still, eyeing the approaching hunter.

Still wondering about his dog, Clark shot the deer. As the animal rolled over in the snow, Clark was astonished to see Old Sound come bounding from beneath the deer's feet, shaking the snow from his coat.

The dog looked downright humiliated as he sat at a safe distance, gazing upon his conqueror in silence. "The cunningest deer" had somehow managed to hold off its canine foe by first beating him into the snow with its forepaws, then deliberately standing on his prostrate body.

BUCKWHEAT AS BIG AS BEECHNUTS

OVER in the Towns of Morehouse and Arietta, in the year 1848, Andrew K. Morehouse was making a last-ditch effort to lure settlers to the vast acreage he had acquired some sixteen years earlier. There had been serious setbacks. As early as 1832, he had tried to found the Village of Bethuneville. Now it existed, an empty shell.

In 1838, he had tried, with even more effort and care, to found the Village of Piseco near the head of Piseco Lake. The success that at first seemed to reward his endeavors had slipped slowly away. The people had become dissatisfied with the deeds he had issued, the titles he had given. One by one, they had slowly departed.

Contributing to his troubles, the dream of a railroad that would cross his lands at length seemed to vanish.

Morehouse, like others before him, had his land alone to offer. The short growing seasons and the rock-strewn soil had long since proved the limited productivity of the mountainous region. Inducement for prospective farmers was small, indeed. Against such a backdrop, Morehouse must make the land appear suitably verdant.

The land-owner used a variety of methods, but without doubt his most famous was to gather a bagful of beechnuts and take them to the docks at New York, where the immigrants were seeking a new home in these prospering United States. Showing the beechnuts as positive proof, Morehouse would tell of the wonderful large kernels of buckwheat being raised on his Southern Adirondack farms.

Many prospective settlers were impressed. On the strength of it, Morehouse began to sell land. But the new arrivals were disappointed to find no such buckwheat-producing fields. Many were anxious to leave forthwith for a more hospitable agricultural climate but could never get enough money ahead to pay their travel fare.

Another method for inducing settlement was to have letters, supposedly written by visitors to the area, reproduced as handouts in New York City. If the glowing accounts therein were not always entirely accurate, they were nonetheless stimulating.

It just happened, it seemed, that three such letters were written within a two-day period.

One letter, dated at Piseco on April 3, 1848, now in the possession of Earl Kreuzer, was supposedly sent by one "A. Burt" to "Mr. Sapher, 99 16th Street, New York City." Morehouse had it printed for all to see.

"Dear Friend," it began. "According to promise, I write you an account of my journey to Hamilton County. We arrived at Utica at 1 A.M. on the 31st. After refreshing ourselves, our party left on foot for Morehouseville, where we arrived the next day.

"On our way, we passed through the Towns of Trenton, Russia, and Ohio. The farmers there appear to live very comfortable. The land generally is pretty good, no high hills. The timber is straight and good and there is but little brush wood.

"On our way, we staid at a farm house occupied by Mr. Tucker, whose wife and family treated us very kindly. We were provided with a good supper and beds; in the morning, after a good breakfast, we proceeded on our journey. The land here is very good, the scenery very beautiful. Mr. Hinckley has near by a fine Saw Mill, with Planing and Floor Plank Machines, capable of carrying on a large business. We arrived at Morehouseville about 2 P.M. Mrs. Morehouse prepared us a good dinner, which we, after our walks, enjoyed very much.

"We conversed with some settlers as we came along, some of them gave us a history of their experience in this country. A minister who has been here nearly four years, has 100 acres of land with two oxen, cows and other live stock. He has a wife and four children. He paid $7 per acre for new land, had only $3 capital to start upon, but by industry and perseverance, is now quite independent. I believe him to be an honest man and his statement may be relied upon.

"Another person, Mr. Cummings, has been located here about twelve years. He told me that when he first came here he had 14 shillings to support his family. He got employment immediately, and occasionally working for himself, he has ultimately established himself, and has a good farm, well stocked and has money in hand. He has a Saw Mill and Grist Mill.

"On Monday our company, consisting of Charles Price, John Lewis, Robert Cochrane, A. Burt, William Boggart, Mr. Morehouse and two Germans, started for Piseco. The land we passed appears equally good as that we had seen on our way to Morehouseville. About six miles from Morehouseville, we came to a Log Cabin, occupied by Messers. Cleverly, Franks and Penny, who have lately settled here. They are perfectly happy and declared that they would not change their situation for the best house in New York.

"We have located on 640 acres on Lots No. 220, 221 and 222 in the Oxbow Tract, Piseco Lake. It is a beautiful place. I think a farm here would suit you, and you would do well to secure it from Mr. M. These lands lay facing to the Sun, and command a fine view of the Lake and surrounding country. The two Germans who came with us intend settling here.

"If you wish to have this letter cross-examined or further information, call upon Robert Cochrane, 163 West 15th St. or John Lewis, foot of 36 Street, North River, as they were of our party and have located with us, but have returned to New York for their families."

The letter deserved the full cross-examination and additional information that its last paragraph solicited. The land the writer proclaimed to have selected for his farm is entirely mountainous, with the high, steep incline coming virtually to the shore of the lake.

Despite such heartening reports from his patrons, despite his own heroic efforts on every front, Morehouse's valiant attempts to bring settlers to the area on a large scale were disappointing. The area lost nothing of the charm of its wilderness setting through undue colonization.

THAT FABULOUS FAMILY
NAMED STURGES

IN A COUNTRY where men are noted for their initiative and independence, old Aaron Sturges was a fabulous character by any standards. Stories of a long series of amazing exploits were told and retold in the mountains many years ago.

Born in 1806, Aaron Sturges was an itinerant shoemaker from Fairfield, Conn. with a curiosity and a wanderlust that decried satiation. His business travels brought him at times to Ballston Spa, where he visited General Sturges, a relative, but his own personal interests brought him to Lake Pleasant.

If business was sparse in the Southern Adirondacks, Aaron found other compensations. He was a rough, primitive type of person; something in his nature responded instinctively to these mountains, their lakes and their forests. Aaron Sturges knew at once that, come what may, this was the place where he must live. The climate would be favorable to his gnawing asthmatic condition, he reasoned; the life of the hunter and trapper intrigued him.

What is more, he must waste no time. Nothing, not even the pregnancy of his young wife, must delay. And so, in early March of 1832, he and Charity Squires Sturges threw their small belongings into a wagon and started, with six-year-old "Burr," on the long trip from Fairfield to Lake Pleasant.

Despite his impatience, a delay was required when the lumbering old wagon reached Cranberry Creek. There it was on March 24th that Charity presented her husband with a baby boy whom they promptly named David. The wagon continued up the road to Northville and into the mountains to Lake Pleasant, while Charity Sturges held the infant David in her arms and the young "Burr" romped and played at the back of the wagon.

Aaron settled his family on fifty acres of land in Lot 22 north of the Corners and promptly set out to make hunting and fishing his career.

"Old Sturge" had been in the mountains only a short time when he had his incredible bout with the devil, not the mental and moral kind of contest that the term usually implies, but a real-life physical encounter.

He had been coached by one of the older woodsmen in setting traps in the Lewey Lake district and now went, rifle in hand, to inspect them. Suddenly, he stiffened as he came upon a huge black beast lying directly on the spot where one of his traps should have been. Never having seen a moose, Aaron Sturges was convinced that this black creature with a bundle of pitchforks and iron-wooden shovels on its head was none other than the "Old Harry" himself.

Completely frightened, his first inclination was to "beat it" for home. More in character, he decided to have a shot at the beast instead. At fairly close range, he blazed away. The creature paid no attention—did not even turn its head.

Somewhat surprised to find himself still alive, Old Sturge hid behind a tree and reloaded. Once more, he fired, without apparent effect of any kind.

Now the hunter was convinced that the strange being bore a charmed life. When he looked down the barrel at the beast, he said it grew "as large as a meeting house." And when, despite his fear, he aimed right at the middle of this great pile, the ball would go completely through, and the hole would close up again.

As Sturge told it, he got madder and madder and worse and worse scared every time he shot. After he had been at it for what he judged to be an hour or two, the great black mass rose and gave one tremendous bound. Sturge heard his steel trap fall clashing against the stones. Then it was gone.

Waiting a decent interval to compose himself, Sturge went to his trap. His worst fears were realized. There, between the saw-like teeth, was a split hoof, the same that Satan was said to have had. Sturge always swore thereafter that there was a strong smell of sulphur in the woods that remained for weeks afterward.

Still frightened, Aaron Sturges brought the hoof into the settlement. The older hunters listened carefully to his story and shook their heads solemnly. No consolation was offered.

When winter came, he went with a party to hunt moose. Suddenly, they came upon a huge bull moose and Sturge was ready to make tracks for home as fast as his snowshoes would carry him.

"That's him! There he is again!" he cried.

With knowing smiles, the huntsmen let him shoot until he brought the moose down. Sturge was able to satisfy himself that it could not be Satan because it lacked the required forked tail.

Sturge killed many moose after that, but never without firing a great many shots. Because, somehow, since that time, he said, they "will look so big I can't see my sights!"

The old Connecticut Yankee was described as a "helter-skelter, harum-scarum, good-natured, headlong fellow, who always managed to blunder into the most unbelievable scrapes with wild animals, yet always had courage enough to come out successfully."

Sturge always kept a number of traps set near Lewey Lake. Coming toward the lake one day with a couple of veteran hunters, he found a large bear caught by the hind leg in one of his traps. Without hesitation, he rushed to it with his hunting knife drawn, ready to cut its throat.

The bear met him with its traditional hug and a desperate struggle began. His companions were too paralyzed with laughter to come to his aid. Sturge finally overcame his furry adversary, but not until all his clothing had been stripped from his body, and he himself was badly torn and bruised.

One day, Old Sturge was trapping alone near Pillsbury. He caught a bear and started to reset his trap, when the sharp-toothed jaws closed on his arm. Nothing could have been more painful. With obdurate courage, he walked for miles out of the woods with the massive trap on his arm.

On another occasion, Old Sturge managed to get into a furious fist-fight with one of his neighbors at Newton's Corners. As the battle mounted to ever greater fury, Sturge was knocked to the ground. Bitterly, he rose to his feet. It was all too apparent that he had acquired a broken arm. Bystanders tried at once to stop the vicious encounter.

Sturge swore mightily and with derision. Despite all protests, he went flailing back to the fray.

Old Sturge ultimately decided that Lewey Lake was by all means the place to be and set out to develop a fishing and hunting camp there. The Town of Lake Pleasant obliged by surveying a road on October 29, 1847 "from the shantee of Aaron Sturges standing on the bank of Lewey Lake to the State road, intersecting said road at a place known as the Hastings Place . . . five miles and 65½ chains." It was the beginning of the new road from Newton's Corners to Indian Lake.

Aaron and his family began to spend more and more of their time there. Well they might. Coming in from Lewey Lake one day, he stopped at the top of Page Hill to show Nate Page a trout he had caught. He had a stick through the fish's gills and carried the stick over his shoulder. Although Sturge was not a tall man, the fish is said to have reached to his heels.

He was pleased to see that, as his sons grew older, they shared his deep interest in the mountains and their forests.

Sturge taught them to walk incredible distances in the mountain wilderness completely on their own, taught them to feel as much at home in the forests as the wild deer they hunted.

Late one season, Sturge had an old horse in the woods at Lewey Lake. There had been an early fall of heavy snow, and the hunter was determined to get the reluctant raw-boned nag to the Corners. His sons were made to carry heavy planks and lay them ahead of the horse for miles so that the animal could walk on the improvised corduroy all the way out of the woods.

As a growing boy, Aaron's oldest son, "Burr," was chopping wood for the kitchen stove one day. An unfortunate glancing stroke of his axe sent the sharp blade through his heavy boot and cut off a substantial chunk of his big toe.

The frightened Burr put up a howl. "I've cut off my toe!" he shouted, as the pain began to swell and the blood started to flow.

Old Sturge strode vigorously out of the house toward his injured son.

"Hm," he murmured as he inspected the severed fragment. "It'll make good bait for mink."

For deeds of prowess, Sturge had everyone stopped. Around Civil War time, he used to hoist a pack basket brimming with lake trout on his shoulders, leave his cabin at Lewey Lake, and walk sixty-five miles to Amsterdam. There he would trade the fish for groceries and walk back the next day. Sometimes, he would be asked to ride in a passing wagon.

"No thanks," he would reply, "I'm in a hurry." And he would out-distance the horses every time. It took a powerful man to keep up with him the last thirteen miles from the Corners to Lewey Lake.

The Sturges family was to be found almost everywhere. As guides, Aaron "Burr" Sturges was most frequently at the Lake Pleasant House, while Dave and Jim made their headquarters at Clark Satterlee's Inn. The opportunity was never lost to bring would-be hunters and fishermen to their father's place at Lewey Lake.

Old Sturge and his wife and daughter were at the Lewey Lake shanty in November, 1858, when Charity Squires Sturges was taken ill and died. There had been a snowfall and Sturge had the job of breaking a way down the lonesome mountain road to the Corners. Leaving his twelve-year-old daughter, Sarah, to take care of the lonely, isolated cabin, he laid his wife's body in the sled and started for town. When he arrived, he built a coffin and had it about completed when he was told that it was not long enough to hold the body.

Sturge thought about it a minute. He had a simple way of righting matters. He simply cut off his wife's legs and placed them beside her in the coffin. He was confident that Charity, with the New England frugality the two had shared in common, would have approved.

Admired as he was for his courage and woodland skills, Sturge was not without his enemies. Before the Civil War, he and John Satterlee (who later went to war and never returned) were trapping and stopped at Sturges' camp beyond Cedar Lake. It was customary to keep provisions in these rough buildings for the use of trappers who might need food. There was evidence that someone had used the camp. Sturge believed it was a trapper from the village with whom he was at odds. The two men made biscuits from flour that was at hand and enjoyed a tasty meal.

As they left, John Satterlee started out ahead and suddenly became violently ill, accusing Sturges of poisoning him. Sturge started at once to chew tobacco and swallow the juice, and made Satterlee do likewise. It saved the two from strychnine poisoning.

Old Sturge continued to live at Lake Pleasant for some years after his wife's death. Then, characteristically, he packed his belongings one day and went back to Fairfield alone. There he died. He is buried in Fairfield.

The hearty tradition of "Old Sturge" was left in capable hands. Each of his sons loved the mountains as much as he. Physical giants, their own strong character made them seem even taller. "Awfully nice companions" was the sportsmen's verdict.

The same is said of the Sturges family represented at Lake Pleasant today.

THE BENAJAH PAGES OF PAGE HILL

HIGH ON THE HILLTOP where the weary, climbing road, with a final lunge, hurls itself across the summit of Page Hill, stands a sizable white-painted house. The view below, over the Village of Speculator, the north end of Lake Pleasant and Speculator Mountain, is breath-taking in its beauty. To the west, the silver shimmer of Sacandaga Lake can be seen above the deep green of the tall and solemn trees.

Here lived the family of Benajah and Sarah Slack Page. Innate dignity and character shone from the features of this grandson of one of Lake Pleasant's earliest settlers throughout his eighty-nine years that began in 1832. Good humor sparkled from his keen blue eyes. Benajah Page was an old guide with many a tale of his hunting to relate.

There was the time when Benage took his dog, "Old Music," into the West Canada country hunting deer. Between Big West and South Lake near South Mountain, he found a fresh track in the newly-fallen snow. The track swung right up South Mountain through the open hardwood timber and the dog could be seen for nearly a mile. Benage watched in admiration as "Old Music" pursued his quest, baying every few jumps. The guide started toward his boat in case the deer should come to the lake, as the deer hound disappeared in a cleft in the mountain.

He was dismayed when the dog's barking turned to a howl of pain. Snarling and sharp barks were heard, then "Old Music" came into view, pursued by two fierce wolves.

Benage yelled at the top of his lungs and fired his gun,

ultimately frightening the wolves away. The dog came hurtling down the mountain, leaving a trail of crimson in the sparkling white snow. When he reached his master, the dog was found bitten through the back of the neck and with a fatal wound just back of the fore-shoulder. A chunk of flesh as big as the hunter's hand had been torn away, laying the lungs bare. The dog lived no longer than an hour. It was one of the few instances where wolves have been known to kill a dog.*

It hurt Benage deeply. Dogs were his friends. He would talk to them as though they were babies. One of his dogs always sat beside him on a chair at the table, and Benage would give his pet a bite of food each time he himself took a spoonful.

Benage enjoyed his social drinking. The neighbors could always tell when he had imbibed. He would open a window in his house and shoot at a target outside. It was the boys' duty to watch how closely he reached his mark.

"Well, Benage is drinking again," the neighbors would say, as the gun blasted mightily away.

Benajah Page is probably best remembered for a verse he composed for a party of unsuccessful hunters. It was a group he had guided before and knew well that he brought out of the woods that hunting season. The men invited their old guide to dine with them at the Sturges House, but Benage told them he had better go home first, but would join them in time to see them off.

It was a convivial group, and when Benage arrived, they promptly ordered him several drinks. Although they had seen and fired on several deer, the hunters had not killed a single deer on their trip.

Warmed to the occasion, Benage sang them a parting song:

> "They do not shoot for money,
> They value not the skin,
> The only thing they shoot 'em for
> Is to see 'em run again."

* From *Forest and Stream*, by M. S. Northrup. Johnstown, N.Y. 1887.

When he died, October 13, 1911, Benajah Page left his name and legend in the hands of a son, little knowing that the younger Page was to give his life to the perpetuation of the family lore.

Benajah Allen Page was just thirty-nine years and eight months old when he took the family wagon to Northville on August 4, 1913 to get provisions. A gregarious person like his father, the younger Benajah stopped at one of the bars in Northville. When he left, he was said to be feeling no pain.

No one worried. The horses were so used to the trip up the old mountain road, the driver had merely to lay the reins on their backs and they would find their way home. They made it, too.

Horses and wagon had passed through Speculator and had started the last leg of their journey up Page Hill. Then it was that Benajah decided that the horses deserved a drink from the open, well-like spring on Page Street, halfway up the ascent. A short time later, the team arrived home without their driver-passenger.

Sarah Page was worried about her son. Perhaps Ralph had better go down to the village and see if he had stopped off at one of the local taverns.

Ralph did not need to travel that far. Halfway down the hill, he found that his brother, Benajah, had fallen into the spring on his head and had drowned.

NEEDLE AND SPOON

A LETTER signed at Piseco by W. D. Jones was sent to Andrew K. Morehouse on March 28, 1847, telling of the changes at the still-existent but rapidly dwindling Village of Piseco.

"H. T. Cronkhite has moved into the Hastings house," it reported. "He has an ox team and cow. I will make him log off some land in spring, work out tax, etc. F. Couch has moved into the Warner house and Mr. F. F. Lobb, tailor, has opened shop at Enos's. W. D. Jones, supervisor; A. Enos, town clerk; T.L. J., assessor and collector and path master; Couch, assessor; Cronkhite and Youmans, commissioners of highways; and next town meeting to be at Piseco. Hurrah for Piseco!"

It is possible that Jones might have been even more exuberant had he realized the full purport of the information his letter contained. New town officers be darned. Floyd Ferris Lobb had come to town.

The mere thought of a tailor setting up shop in a rural area like Piseco is reason for wonder. The townspeople at Piseco wondered, too. But Floyd F. Lobb was adamant on the subject.

"I'm F. F. Lobb, tailor, by God," he would affirm. No one was to doubt the fact.

A veteran fisherman, trapper and woodsman, the Pennsylvania-born migrant was eventually to place a sign over the doorway of his hut, reading: "Lobbville." Even today the name of Lobbville is occasionally applied to the group of summer camps on the northwest side of Piseco Lake.

Old Lobb first lived in an open-front bark shanty, then in a small wooden hut. He was a slight little man, who always seemed ageless. In later years, he was extremely deaf, and the only way to be understood was to shout in his ear. He had a thin, squeally little voice. It was after the death of his wife that he began his solitary existence.

William P. Courtney was one of Lobb's neighbors. Courtney kept geese and Lobb kept turkeys. Lobb's turkeys had the unfortunate habit of wandering into their neighbor's yard, a fact that Courtney found most irritating. One day, he gave Lobb a solemn promise that if he did not keep his turkeys at home, they would be shot. The eccentric Lobb paid no attention.

Shortly after, true to his word, Courtney shot a very fine gobbler. Lobb picked up his own gun and shot one of Courtney's ganders that was wandering in the road. Then, he turned to Courtney with the words:

"An eye for an eye and a tooth for a tooth,
You killed my turkey, and I'll kill your goose."

Lobb invented a fishing spoon that was favored for many years by trout fishermen. It was considered the best of its day. Known as the "Lobb Spoon" or "Old Lobb Bait," it is still in use.

Old Lobb brought his father, Isaac, to Piseco in 1884, and Isaac was drowned in the lake. After that, Lobb would never hunt or fish on Sundays.

His profession was fishing and he spent a great deal of time at his fishing buoy on the lake, as well as trolling the lake for trout. He was known to sit at his anchor with his back to the west when a thunderstorm brewed. Being so deaf, he heard no thunder. Sometimes the wind would strike and the mounting waves would tear him away from his mooring, sending him swooping some distance down the lake before he could regain control.

If he liked a person, he treated him well. If he did not, he never failed to tell him so. Newcomers to Piseco Lake were likely to be greeted with, "You better go home; your mother needs you for soap grease."

Lobb used to say that, when he died, he would like to be buried on nearby Panther Mountain, an impressive spot with a magnificent view. His deep love for fishing caused another strange request that his friends and neighbors were able to fulfill. When he realized that his last days were near, he sent for an old friend, Charles J. Seavey of Poland, N.Y., and in utter seriousness, made Seavey promise faithfully to bury with him a complete fishing outfit.

One day in 1890, George and Martha Aldous Rudes, who lived across the waters of Piseco at the community of Spy Lake, remarked that they had not seen old Lobb for some time. George and his boys decided to row across the lake to investigate.

They found Lobb in his cabin, seriously ill. Not wanting to

leave him helpless and alone, the Rudes persuaded the old fisherman to come to their home at Spy Lake.

Lobb was willing. He was loaded onto a mattress and placed in the boat. But, realizing how sick he was, he made an earnest request. He would like to catch just one more lake trout before he died.

A line was rigged, and a Lobb spoon attached. During the slow trip across the lake, the old hermit trolled. A smile lighted his pale, wan, weatherbeaten face when happily he caught two lake trout.

The next day, Old Lobb died at George Rudes' home. When he was laid to rest in the little Higgins Bay Cemetery on the east side of the lake, he took with him to the Happy Fishing Grounds of the Beyond a rod, reel, lines, hooks, and several of the trolling spoons he had created. His is an unmarked grave.

Perhaps to Lobb, more than to any other, goes the application of the words of the anonymous "Fisherman's Prayer": *

"God grant that I may live to fish until my dying day,
And when it comes to my last cast, I then most humbly pray,
When in the Lord's safe landing net, I'm peacefully asleep,
That in His Mercy, I be judged as good enough to keep."

LAST MOOSE IN THE MOUNTAINS

THE ANCIENT big-horned moose that abounded in the Adirondacks in the first half of the century had virtually disappeared by 1858. They left a lot of legend behind.

It was a cold winter day when Silas B. Call and Henry Courtney started on a hunting trip far into the Moose River country. Nearing their destination, they separated, each hoping to scare up game. Henry Courtney was fortunate enough to

* Published in *The New York Conservationist.* Issue of February–March. 1953.

find a moose, which he killed at once. Promptly, he skinned the animal. The wind was icy cold as he proceeded with his work. He needed warmth. What better way than to make use of the materials at hand?

Courtney wrapped himself in the still-warm skin of the moose and lay down out of the gale to have a nap before starting home. When at length he was fully rested and ready to begin the journey, he found he had encountered a major problem. Where the flesh of the moose clung to the fur, it had frozen solid and he could not get out. He was trapped by his own ingenuity.

Silas Call reached home that blustery night and waited in vain for his companion. Certain that an accident had occurred, he was back on the trail early the following morning, retracing Courtney's foot-prints in the snow.

After miles of hiking, Sil Call came upon a peculiar sight. There was his good friend Courtney lying on the snowy ground, unable to move. He was comfortable enough, sufficiently warm. But wrapped in the moose's skin, he was helpless.

Call took his hunting knife and cut his friend loose. They returned to the village, where subsequent listeners were never quite able to classify their story as tall tale or true.

About the same time, William Courtney, proprietor of a hotel at Piseco, took his son trapping one winter near Spruce Lake. Suddenly, they came upon a small moose seemingly trapped in the snow. Moose had become a rarity in the Adirondacks, although hardly more scarce than money. The two decided to bring the moose out alive. They could sell it to a small park in Saratoga, the owners of which had offered to pay twenty-five dollars for such an animal. But first, the moose must be delivered.

The two Courtneys took their axes and felled trees around the animal to make a fence. Throughout the remainder of the winter, father and son, with a patience born of promise, took turns in staying on the premises. Painstakingly, the moose was fed. Diligently, it was tamed. They were even able to break it to lead.

Spring came with all its promise. It was time to drive the moose from the woods and start it down the long, long road. The trip proved difficult, but at last they were virtually in sight of their goal.

Outside of Saratoga, some eighty miles from the point of capture, several dogs appeared. With savage barking, they charged after the animal. Thoroughly frightened, the moose bolted and got away. When it was found, only a lifeless carcass remained. A winter's diligent labor had gone in vain.

* * * * *

George Youmans, a man of short stature, was a hunter and trapper of the Piseco area for many years. Muskrat pelts brought from four to eight cents at that time.

Youmans and Charles Letson had a trap line from Piseco to the West Canada Lake country. While walking the line one day, a serious disagreement over strategy arose at West Canada Lake. For hours, they hiked together in animated discussion until, at long last, they reached sight of home.

Still unable to come to a reconciliation of views, they turned right around again and hiked the many rough miles back to West Canada to settle the argument, a distance of eighteen miles each way.

LAKE PLEASANT'S POT OF GOLD

BACK IN 1861, when the terrible storm of Civil War swept over the growing nation and men were being called to their country's service, the able-bodied men of Lake Pleasant began to gird for defense.

Practice drilling was undertaken on the rolling ground of

the Charles Letson farm, where the road to Moffitt's Beach joins the Speculator-Lake Pleasant highway on the north shore of the lake. The large elm tree that still stands near the field was hung with targets for rifle practice.

Preparations were being made for those who would be called to service. But, as the months moved on, preparations were being made for possible defense. Older residents remembered the enemy strikes into upper New York State from Canada during the War of 1812. No one could be sure it would not happen again. Ultimate proof that the apprehension was not wholly ill-founded was given in 1864, when on October 19th the town of St. Albans, Vermont, about 15 miles from the Canadian frontier, was raided by armed Confederates, who overpowered the employees of three banks, fired on and killed several persons, and stole $200,000 in money, taking all the horses they could find.

Perhaps it was to comfort a child, frightened by the shots fired around the old elm tree on the Letson farm, that a legend grew. But it has persisted for generations, been retold again and again, and has lived to the present day.

The simple story tells that a pot of gold lies buried beneath the old elm tree. In order to obtain this gold, one must dig until the pot comes into view, then toss coins upon it and the gold will appear.

One warning, however. One must not speak or laugh during the procedure, or the gold will vanish, pot and all.

There is no record of anyone's having actively gone after this mythical treasure.

The Town of Lake Pleasant that had sent forty men to its country's service, nine of whom were never to return, could use a light-hearted legend of this kind.

THEY WENT TO WAR

THE TIDES of Civil War that did much to change the face of Hamilton County made a marked change in the appearance of Chet Sturges. One of three of old Aaron Sturges' sons to serve, Chet had joined his brother, Alfred, in hiking through the dense woods to Indian Lake from their father's log cabin on Lewey Lake to enlist on July 25, 1862 in Company C, 93rd Infantry. They were following in the footsteps of their brother, Lewis, who had signed up with Company C, 22nd Infantry Regiment at Glens Falls the previous November.

Chet was twenty-three and Al was seventeen the day they stuffed their meager belongings in burlap bags, slung them over their shoulders, and started up the dusty road from Lewey Lake. Old Aaron, never one for sentiment, stood outside the cabin, looking after them.

"Bring me back my sacks full of onions!" he called. It was his parting remark to sons due to be away for three years.

The hardy Sturges boys returned, all three of them. But Chet never looked quite the same. During the Battle of the Wilderness, he was sighting his rifle across the limb of a tree when he was struck in the jaw with a bullet.

Chet lay helpless for three days. His face was full of maggots, a condition that probably saved his life. When at length he was rescued and had recovered from his wound, the scar remained ugly and deep. Chet always wore whiskers after that to hide his disfigurement.

It was during the same Battle of the Wilderness that Dave Satterlee gained his firm belief in premonition.

Dave used to tell that, as the men rolled out of their blankets one morning, his cousin turned to him thoughtfully.

"Today is my day," he told Dave positively. Pointing to a

spot midway between his nose and upper lip, he added, "I'm going to get it right here."

That day as the battle raged, Dave's cousin was hit in the mustache by a bullet as big as your thumb. His lower face was shattered; his condition was grave. He died of yellow fever in a hospital in Philadelphia, where he had been taken for treatment of the wound.

Dave Satterlee had just turned twenty-one when he and his brother, John, five years Dave's senior, went over to the old white-painted wooden courthouse at Lake Pleasant on August 28, 1862 and signed up with the 4th New York Heavy Artillery. A total of eight Lake Pleasant residents enlisted that day—George Burton, Jack Gibbs, Robert Hawkins, George Letson, Philip Monk, Abram R. Parslow, and the Satterlee boys. With them was Cyrus Dunham of the Town of Hope.

Bob Hawkins was wounded and died in a hospital in Washington. The rest had come along all right—that is, until they were down on the Weldon Railroad outside of Petersburg, Virginia.

Three companies of Union soldiers were at work tearing up the railroad to prevent its use by the Southerners, Dave Satterlee told. They would rip up the ties and burn them, placing the rails in the hot flames until they were pliable enough to be bent around trees and destroyed.

Suddenly, a detachment of Southern cavalry surprised the Northern troops and made a charge. The men barely had time to grab their guns.

The initial charge was made on Dave's outfit and the line was held. A second, more violent, attack followed in the same sector. Again, the enemy was repulsed.

The third charge was made on the company of Pennsylvania Dutchmen on the right. The men broke and ran, leaving an exposed company flank. Dave's company was surrounded and forced to surrender.

The Northerners were given a choice of prisons to which they might be sent. It wasn't much of a choice though, because the soldiers had heard well of how tough the Southern prisons could be.

Dave elected to go to Belle Island in the James River above Richmond. John Satterlee chose Andersonville. Dave stood watching as the elder John was marched off with the straggling group of demoralized boys in blue. He was never to see his brother again.

On Belle Island, the men were yarded on an open sandy flat land, with guards on both sides of the river. Food was poor and hopelessly insufficient. Medical care was non-existent and sanitary conditions left much to be desired. The place was wracked with dysentery, yellow fever and a variety of other diseases. The men were dying so fast, the bodies couldn't be carted away fast enough and were left in huge piles on the shore. Dave became so weak from starvation, he couldn't walk.

Relief came as Grant's forces advanced on the north side of the James River to within seven miles of Richmond. The prisoners' releases were arranged.

Dave was carried off Belle Island on a stretcher. Looking up weakly, he recognized his litter bearers as his old friends, Cy Dunham, who later lived in Arietta, and Phil Monk, who ultimately settled on the west bank of the Sacandaga River in Hope and served for several years as coroner of Hamilton County.

Not long afterward, Dave arrived home to find his family decimated by smallpox, the home farm abandoned, and himself and his seventeen-year-old brother, Barber, the sole support.

THE EPIDEMIC OF 1865

THE WAR had been a brutal thing for Emiline Gallup. It had struck early and close. Almost three years had passed since that terrible day in April, 1862. Yet she remembered every detail.

Again, she was rising before dawn and stirring the dying coals in the fireplace to new life. The children were called. Seventeen-year-old Frances was leaving, after a hurried breakfast, for her work as domestic at the Courtney home. Henry, age 15, was at work in the barn on their little farm. Hiram, 14, and nine-year-old Martha were off to school at the corners. At length the day had started and Emiline Gallup was alone.

It had been barely six months since George Gallup had left for military service with the 34th Infantry Regiment, but the resultant added responsibility to her family, in her husband's absence, had become routine.

She busied herself with a thousand tasks that morning—the baking of bread, the spinning of flax, mending the boys' clothing. Yet all the time her ears were alert for sounds in the deep-rutted, mucky road. It was mail day and the expected letter from her husband was long overdue.

She heard the rattle of the wagon, the whinnying of the horses, and finally the call of old Ben Gallup, as he brought the team to a halt. Anxiously, she had rushed to the door to greet her elderly father-in-law with questioning face. Had the awaited letter come at last?

There was a graveness in old Ben's manner as he entered the house. She thought she saw his hand tremble a little as he handed her the yellow envelope from the Department of War. With determination, she opened the official letter and stood staring at its message, reading it over and over, unable to comprehend. Wordlessly, she passed it to George's father.

They were meaningless words, those official regrets. Hand-written in beautiful script by an army clerk's punctilious hand, they told of things she could not, would not understand. It wasn't true. George hadn't died of illness in a New York City hospital. It simply wasn't fair.

Old Ben had sat with her a while, discussing every aspect of the fateful message. Helplessly, he had told her again about his father's service in the Revolution, and about the old army rifle that still hung above the fireplace in his own small house. Once her eyes had started to fill with tears, but she had quickly brushed them away. Finally, it was her father-in-law who remembered to call young Henry from the barn.

Emiline saw her fifteen-year-old son come sauntering to the door. She saw his welcoming smile change to an expression of inquiry. Suddenly, she was choked with emotion that would not still.

"He's so young," she thought, "so very, very young." And she rushed to him, threw her arms about his shoulders, and shook with uncontrollable sobs.

There was another such dark day in the early weeks of 1864, when Ben and Lana Gallup received the message that a second son, Hiram, had died a hero's death on the battlefield. The family was deeply saddened. Emiline was stunned. Quietly, she knelt to the floor and prayed that the last son, still in service, would be spared by a just and understanding God.

And it happened! In late November of 1864, William C. Gallup, late soldier in his country's armed forces, returned home, his three-year enlistment completed. Happily, Emiline ran to him with arms outflung and a sister-in-law's welcoming kiss on his cheek.

For a moment, she felt a cruelly wrenching pang as she stepped back to survey the newly-discharged soldier. It was just four years ago that George had left.

William Gallup was thin and weakened, Emiline saw. His face seemed pale and wan. It was then she learned that he had recently left the hospital after illness from smallpox. But he's home now, and that's all that matters, she thought joyfully, and began hasty plans with Mother Lana for a family feast.

For an instant, she remembered that the Satterlees down the road had had no word about their son, John, since that brief letter from the War Department telling them that he had been taken prisoner and must be presumed dead. David Satterlee was still in service, she remembered. She made a quick resolve to pay them a visit during the holidays. She must remind William to do the same.

The family dinner that was repeated again at Christmas time was a happy occasion, yet a happiness framed in sadness. Emiline knew that things would never be the same again. Nonetheless, these were holidays to be remembered, holidays for which to be grateful.

And then it struck!

Young Hiram became sick first. Emiline treated him for fever and cold, but he only seemed to grow steadily worse. Then, in quick succession, each of the other children developed the same symptoms. And as their conditions worsened, the doctor from down the county was called. To the abject horror of herself and the community at large, the sickness was pronounced the dreaded smallpox by Dr. Levi Sabin, and the helpless family was quarantined to its home.

In the grave emergency, the whole community responded. The new Town Board of Health took charge and directed the delivery of groceries, the cutting of wood, the necessary chores. Henry A. Parslow and William Gallup worked with a will.

When Emiline herself was taken sick, Catherine Morrison was sent from Wells to remain at the house under quarantine for three weeks. Without Catherine, it would have been impossible to get along.

Henry Courtney, as Overseer of the Poor, the only town officer in a position to offer help, made a two-day trip to Wells. Supplies were ordered from the stores of William Burnham & Son and Sampson Hosley of Wells, and from the store of

Charles Bidwell of Lake Pleasant. Aaron Snell was called into service for seven days of work about the Gallup Farm.

The disease continued to rage. For three bleak months, it persisted. Finally, in March, it left the Gallup home, and the community breathed a sigh of relief.

The respite was of short duration. Once more, the plague struck with fury, this time about two miles down the south shore road at the hilltop home of Selah and Mariah Dodge Satterlee.

Once more the community responded. Dr. Levi Sabin was called to heroic service. The Town Board of Health ordered groceries, toweling, muslin, sugar, saleratis, nails, matches, candles, and "cloth for pants" from William Burnham & Son of Wells. Further supplies of flour, potatoes and plank were purchased from the Lake Pleasant store of Silas Call. House-wives baked bread and pastry. All were delivered to the door-yard to be carried into the stricken house by family members.

Word that leaked from the shuttered household was omi-nous. Not only were the lives of Sarah and Betsey, the two youngest daughters, endangered, but Selah Satterlee himself was gravely ill.

In quick succession, the two daughters passed away and were quietly buried at night-time on the family farm. Then, in a crowning tragedy, the death of Selah Satterlee occurred in this April of 1865.

It was the wish of the family that he be buried in the new village cemetery across the lake at Newton's Corners. But the Board of Health rejected the idea as entirely too hazardous for the community's health. Thomas Ronalds of Wells, the cabinet-maker from Scotland, was hastily recruited to furnish "one coffin and box for Mr. Selah Satterlee," for which he was later paid thirteen dollars. Under the direction of Henry Courtney, the body was taken out of the house under cover of darkness that same night and buried in an unmarked grave in the Peck family cemetery on the south side of the lake.

Emiline Gallup, for her part, went to the Satterlee home,

after the scourge had passed, and devoted four full days to thoroughly cleaning and whitewashing the little house.

Four months later, young David Satterlee, age 23, arrived home from war-time service to find a decimated, desolate family, his father dead from smallpox, his brother dead in the service, and the family homestead placed for sale. Only his mother, his sister Mary, and his seventeen-year-old brother, Barber, now living in a small cottage near the outlet of Lake Pleasant, remained from a once sizable family group.

TALL TALES ARE BORN

No ONE KNOWS who originated the famous tall tales of the Adirondacks. Yet some responsibility to the Greenfields, Abner and his son, William, certainly accrues.

Everyone claimed the Greenfields. They lived, in truth, for a time in Gilmantown in the Town of Wells, later moving to a small cabin near the junction of the Saratoga, Fulton and Hamilton County lines. They lived, in untruth, throughout the entire Southern Adirondacks, where they frequently hunted and where the stories of their unusual adventures were constantly being told.

It seems that Abner Greenfield took his gun one day and went hunting partridges in the Town of Wells. He walked and walked until he reached a lake and decided to sit down and rest. Suddenly, he spied a dozen partridges perched on a big pine limb overhanging the water. He poised his gun, ready to shoot the largest bird, when an idea gave him pause. If he shot one bird, the others would fly away; but if he shot the limb and split it, the birds' toes would be caught in the crack, and he could get all twelve.

Abner shot the limb, caught all the birds by their toes, then had to wade out for the limb, which had fallen into the lake.

Water filled his boots and trouser legs, but he retrieved the limb with its captured game and wallowed toward shore. When he climbed out of the water, he found his trouser legs were full of fish. The weight was so great that a button popped off his suspenders, flew forty rods and killed a rabbit.

Abner was near the mill house on Gilman Lake one day when his dog began to bark. Quickly, he grabbed his gun and sighted on a huge buck. He pulled the trigger, but the gun misfired. Abner peered down the barrel and saw the bullet coming. He had to get that gun barrel down fast and back on target in order to bag that deer.

Abner was lucklessly trapping muskrats one spring on the Kunjamuck. He just couldn't seem to get them into his traps; the small animals would merely sit and eye him with curiosity. Abner had to fire his gun, then grab the "rats" and hold them in place so that they could be hit by the bullets.

It was early spring, too, when Abner was fishing on Mud Lake. The trout were leaping like crazy, but couldn't be made to take bait. Suddenly, it turned bitterly cold and a glaze of ice hardened over the lake's surface. The elder Greenfield found that the fish had frozen in mid-leap, their heads buried in the ice, bodies protruding in the air. All he had to do was walk on the ice and kick off their heads to catch a nice mess.

There was a pinnacle near the Greenfield house and Abner climbed it with a group of visitors. From the top, you could see way down toward Albany. With a wink to his companions, one of the men asked his host if he could see a fly climbing on a white church steeple barely visible in the distance.

Abner squinted hard and long. "No, I can't see him," he affirmed at length, "but I can hear him walking."

All such experiences pale when compared to the time that Abner went out hunting bear. The bear got pretty upset at the intrusion, it seems, and before it was over, the maddened beast had torn out much of Abner's insides. This was a mighty dangerous situation. Abner hastily gathered them up, shoved them in the long deep incision, and held his hand over his abdomen as he hurried home.

His wife had just finished killing a sheep when Abner reached their little cabin up the road toward Lou Tenant's, and the sheep's entrails were all over the chopping block. As he reached the scene, the pressure was too much for Abner. Gasping, he fell against the block and out came his innards once more.

Together, he and his wife managed to gather them up and sew them inside. It was a close call for Abner but, being a strong physical specimen, he recovered.

That was by no means the end of the incident. The following spring, his wife gave birth to twin lambs.

A neighbor once found the elder Greenfield cutting wood near Harris Lake in the Town of Hope.

"Abner, tell me a good lie," he begged.

"Can't," replied Abner. "Haven't got time. My brother just cut his leg over in the woodlot and I'm on my way to Northville for a doctor."

The alarmed neighbor hastened to the spot and found Abner's brother hale and hearty and happily at work.

Bill Greenfield was born in 1830 and, as he grew toward manhood, it became evident that he, too, was to have experiences every bit as startling as those of his parent. Matter of fact, they used to say in the Town of Hope that Abner Greenfield only had one son who took after him and he took after him with a double-bitted axe. Ultimately it was agreed that Bill killed Abner by telling a bigger lie than his dad.

Bill Greenfield was out hunting one day in early spring. Now, the mosquitoes can get mighty thick sometimes in the Town of Hope when the insect mating season is at hand. "They were really putting it to him," as one man tells.

Unable to stand the punishment longer, Bill got under one of the huge heavy iron kettles then used at the tanneries at Hope Falls, and turned it over his head. Furiously, the enraged mosquitoes dive-bombed the metal protector and drove their stingers right through the iron kettle. Each time, Bill would clinch them there with a stone. And, you know, it wasn't long before the mosquitoes lifted that iron kettle right off Bill's body and flew away with it clear over the mountain and out of sight.

When men used to go over to Bill's cabin, there was always a necessary preliminary.

"Wait a minute until I trip the gun," he would say. "It'll blow a man to pieces."

Neighbors soon learned that it was merely a part of the ritual and waited patiently while Bill tripped the non-existent firing piece.

Bill used to tell that his cabin had two stories, one story up and one story down. It was said that the only furnishings were stove, bed, and chairs arranged around a table, where the most important piece of all, the checkerboard, lay. Decorations in the main room were untold numbers of wishbones which Bill claimed came from the chickens he had eaten.

When a neighbor once asked how he was getting along with his haying, Bill had a ready reply.

"Fine," he replied. "We've stacked all we could outside and put the rest in the barn."

To hear him tell it, the old hermit kept some unusual fowls and animals around his place. There were turkeys so tall they could pick the fruit off the trees, and a dog so smart that it once taught school.

Checker-playing was a passion with Bill Greenfield. On one occasion, he "changed work" with a man at Edinburg, helping him put in hay. Later, the man went over to Bill's house to return the favor. For hours on end, Bill kept his friend playing checkers. Finally, concerned over the work that must certainly lie in wait, the man suggested that they quit and get to business.

"Listen," Greenfield told him. "When I was down to your place, I did what you wanted. When you're at my place, you do the same."

An expert at the game, this Paul Bunyan of the Adirondacks

was reputed to have owned two sets of checkers—one of ten-dollar gold pieces and the other of five. These he carefully guarded, and only lost one game in his life. It happened at the hands of Lou Tenant and the local doctor, who engineered a scheme to beat Bill at his own game. Their secret was never learned. Even Bill's eyeglasses, which he always claimed were so strong he could see through a rock ten feet thick, did not help him to discover their trick.

Bill used to buy powder by the keg for his old muzzle-loader gun. One day, he arrived home in a thunderstorm with only a half-filled container. It was a bad one, he told his neighbors. Lightning had struck the keg and burned up half the powder before he could put out the fire. No one disputed the story, even when it was learned from the store-keeper that Bill's thriftiness had caused him to buy only half a keg that day.

The time finally came when Bill felt he should part with his old muzzle-loader. Constantly, he tried to sell it to a neighbor with the claim that it was worth much more than the price. After many refusals, the neighbor was finally worn by the persuasion and agreed to the purchase. As he watched, amazed, Bill removed several gold coins from a secret compartment in the gun stock. There was the proof, he explained, that the gun was worth more than the bargaining price.

Before his death, Bill let it be known that he had a hoard of gold and Civil War pension money carefully buried in a secret location. He never revealed the spot. Even now, treasure seekers are said to search up and down the hills and valleys for Greenfield's buried gold.

"Big Shot" Bill Greenfield died in 1903 at the age of 70 and was supposed to have been buried in an expensive rosewood casket. A distrustful relative later had the coffin exhumed, to find, as suspected, that it was a cheap pine box. The relative is said to have insisted that the undertaker reduce his bill.

The tall-tale hero of the Southern Adirondacks is buried in the Clarksville Cemetery near Edinburg. His small cabin has long since disintegrated with the passing years. Only the foundation remains; the hedgehogs have eaten away the floor.

But the legends of Abner and Bill Greenfield will always endure while mountain men still gather around hearth or campfire to swap Adirondack yarns.

BIDWELL'S HOTEL

JOEL NEWTON had started his village at the corners above the outlet of Lake Pleasant. His own store and small hotel were in operation on the southeast corner from 1840 until the building was destroyed by fire in 1870. The Newton's Corners Post Office had been established there on December 8, 1864.

Clark Satterlee's farm and small inn were located above the corners on the road toward Indian Lake. Nearby, in the 1850's, was the store of Aaron "Burr" Sturges. By 1870, Clark was running the general store, deeding it to his son, Toles, in 1877. It was the typical country store of the community, handling such staples as flour, pork, brown sugar, green tea, dried apples and corn meal.

Dave Sturges had opened his new Sturges House in 1859 across from Clark Satterlee's home.

In the center of the crossroads was a small park. Trees shaded the benches along the walks that led to the village pump, a natural place of congregation in balmy weather. Near the center of the park was a large boulder with a surveyor's mark placed by the State surveyor, Verplanck Colvin, indicating that Newton's Corners stood 30 feet above the level of the lake, 1725 feet above sea level.

The main stage route came up the West River road from Wells, past Hamilton Lake, and directly to Lake Pleasant Village, but the people of Newton's Corners used the old military road to travel to Northville and Wells.

There was one hotel in the area that had housed one brief sojourner. Charles Bidwell, the mason and sometimes merchant, was driving his team and sleigh up the old State road from Wells with the mail one night when he was caught in a severe blizzard. The road was becoming clogged with drifts and visibility was impossible through the driving, wind-whipped snow. It was suicide to continue up the road, yet there was no house for miles.

About two miles below Newton's Corners, Charlie Bidwell came upon the huge cleft rock that stands beside the road. It was his only chance.

Charlie drove his team and sled between the wide split in the rock and lay down to sleep in the sheltered wagon.

The storm passed. The next day was sunny, and Bidwell and his team pushed their way into the settlement. When his story was told, the cleft rock was promptly termed "Bidwell's Hotel," a name that it retains today.

Some seventy-five years later, the indefatigable Pants Lawrence added his own embellishment to the location's lore. Pants told a city sportsman that his grandfather had used the huge rock atop Bidwell's Hotel to crack butternuts, and had forgotten and left it there.

THE CHURCH IS GONE

THE APPEALS of Andrew K. Morehouse to foreign-born, as they reached America's shores, to settle in his mountain community in the 1830's and thereafter, early met the ears of an idealistic Frenchman. The recent immigrant to New York City decided on settlement in Morehouse. He would encourage others of his countrymen to follow. Here, they would carve farms from the wilderness. Here, they would raise their families. The promise of America would be realized in the beautiful mountain town.

The Frenchman came to the Town of Morehouse to fulfill his glowing ambitions. In a burst of enterprise and spirit, he bought land, erected a fine house, built fences, opened roads. His own tidy farm was encouragement for further French families to follow. Most of all, his attention was centered around the building of a needed Roman Catholic Church for the people he had induced to settle in the town.

The man, now believed to have been Joseph Pelletier, commonly known as Petchie, gave the land in reverence and saw his ambitions flower in the construction of a white-painted church with trim, green-painted shutters. A small Catholic cemetery surrounded the substantial building. In it, Pelletier reserved a small plot of ground for the burial, at life's termination, of himself and his wife.

Sheds to house the horses and carriages of the attending congregation were at the rear. Prim flowers lined the walk to the stone steps leading into the sanctuary. A white rail fence surrounded the entire plot. Joesph Pelletier, if such he was, could look upon the church his means had fostered with satisfaction supreme.

The church grew and prospered for several years. Father John U.A. Herbst, born in Holland in 1818, had been summoned to Morehouseville prior to 1850 with his family, to become its pastor. He was a stolid person, severe in his own personal approach to life, stern in his determination that his parishioners adhere strictly to the tenets of their faith. His was a cold personality and, although he won wide respect among his congregation, he gained few friends. Herbst's was a personality that cast a chill on any personal warmth demonstrated in his behalf.

Gradually, a change took place in Pelletier, the benefactor of the Morehouse Roman Catholic Church. A morose spirit superseded his charitable character. An untold irritability settled over his customary good nature. The drinking habit, which had started in a limited way, became almost overpowering. A troubled marital life soon followed.

One dark and brooding night in about the year 1866, the aging Frenchman lurched into his house, angered by drink. Harsh words soon led to cruel accusations between himself and his wife. In the oppressive silence that followed, Joseph stumbled heavily to his feverish bed. Deeply injured, his beleaguered wife stole away to the barn. The next morning, her body was found dangling at the end of a fatal rope.

The sympathetic townspeople were appalled as they prepared the woman's burial. All arrangements for the funeral had been completed when the church parishioners were shocked to learn that their pastor was less than enthusiastic. The priest categorically refused a church service for the woman, due to the manner of her death. Such was forbidden by the rules of the church. Hers was flagrant evidence of sin. To permit normal church burial would be to flaunt all rules, both of ritual and of decency. To forbid such burial would serve as an object lesson to those who might be similarly tempted.

The anger of the congregation mounted. The affront was being made to the founder of the church and his family. Without him, the church would not even exist. As the matter was discussed from neighbor to neighbor, the people rose up in arms. In a final burst of fury, a representative group visited the pastor with a firm ultimatum. The woman would be permitted religious service and decent burial within her own faith.

Faced with an array of wills as stolid as his own, the priest submitted. A church service and a Christian burial were administered. At the close, the troubled priest called the members together in front of the church. Angrily, he flung himself to the door and locked the edifice.

"For the wicked act of yours, I lock this church," he cried, "and lock the devil inside. The key is in my pocket."

Shortly, the disgruntled pastor left the community, never again to be seen in the mountain region. The superstitious congregation would never again enter the sanctuary. Gradually, they moved away, until hardly a French Catholic was left in Morehouseville.

Uncle Dave Sturges, proprietor for sixty-two years of the well-known Sturges House at Newton's Corners.

The David Isdell House in Hope. First stone house in Hamilton County.

By the late 1870's, the church was fast crumbling away. The grounds, where formerly stood the sheds and outbuildings, became a low, damp marsh. Weeds pushed hard against the dilapidated rail fence and the flowering hedges fell into wilderness state. The once proud white church edifice turned gray and weather-beaten. The stone steps grew slippery with moss. Black crows and inquisitive night owls nested in the belfry where the silver-throated bell that once called people to their morning devotions was rusting and powdering with disuse. Within, the simple altar and oaken crucifix became worm-eaten and decayed.

An adventurous group of city sportsmen once flung open the door to view his Satanic majesty. They were greeted by a lightning-fast whirring of wings as a dark shadow passed out the door.

The veil of the passing years has long since dimmed the names of the actors in the grim drama. The hopes, the effort, the hardship that went into the building of the edifice have been erased by five-score years. Only the bare outlines of the tragedy are shown in the few white gravestones in the semblance of an enclosure that remain. The Roman Catholic Church of Morehouse is no more.

THE MAKING OF A GUIDE

IN THE LATTER YEARS of the nineteenth century, summer visitors began to invade the Southern Adirondacks with new enthusiasm and full determination to enjoy all that the mountains afforded. Recreation became a new business.

Visitors had their choice of several hotels of varying size in the Lake Pleasant area, but if a real flavor of the community was the goal, the inevitable choice was the Sturges House at Newton's Corners. "The proprietor," said *Wallace's Guide to the Adirondacks,* "belongs to a family of noted hunters." It was virtual understatement.

Almost from the time they were able to walk, David Sturges and his brothers were in the woods with their father. In their early teens, when boys elsewhere in American cities and villages were tossing baseballs on vacant lots, the Sturges boys were guiding hunting or fishing parties deep into the woodlands.

One day in late October, about the year 1841, when young Dave was about eight years old, his father took him on what promised to be an eight-day trip into the woods to set traps. With them, they took a tired old nag, intending to kill the recalcitrant animal and use its flesh for trap bait. Mink, marten and otter were their quest and such a trip could net anywhere from ninety-eight to two hundred and thirty-eight dollars in pelts after October 20th, when the fur is ready.

Just before they reached the Sturges shanty, they were surprised to find a lone and silent man sitting propped against a protective tree. Closer inspection proved that he had been dead for some hours.

Old Aaron instructed young Dave to stay right there while he trudged back to the village to notify the authorities. Here was a good opportunity to earn some extra money while performing a good deed, the old Yankee reasoned.

For two days, the eight-year-old remained alone with the corpse and the seedy old horse. He ate from the provisions left in the camp and picked cranberries growing nearby. At night, he built a fire to scare away the wolves that were so plentiful in that country at the time, tearing the bark from the back of his father's shanty to keep the flames alive. Meantime, the old horse had fallen and was unable to rise to his feet again.

Young Dave cried himself to sleep. He was not afraid. He was merely plain lonesome.

When at last his father returned with the justice of the peace from Lake Pleasant, they tried without success to determine the dead man's identity. He was, it appeared, some itinerant German who, in his travels, had stopped to rest by the tree before he had died. Together, the men dug a grave and buried the corpse. And from that day to this, the location has been known as Manbury Mountain.

Old Sturge received two dollars for his service to the township. He was appalled. There was an explosive term in the heartiest of mountain tradition. "The next man I find, I'll cut him up for sable bait," he vowed.

There is a story told as fact by older residents of the area that Aaron once sold young Dave to the Indians of the area. The boy was gone for two years. A squaw brought him to a clearing in the woods and showed him the escape route home. Dave watched the sun for directions and made it safely into the village. True or not, it is certain that Aaron once sent the child alone on a long junket to Indian Lake to get honey from the Indians.

When he was twelve years old, young Dave was packed away to Fairfield, Conn. to live with Banks Sturges, his grandfather, and receive formal school training. Dave remained until he was seventeen, taking cruises on his grandfather's sloop from New London to New York City during vacations. At Fairfield, he encountered the family traditions—that J. Pierpont Morgan had married a Sturges and had given the bell to the Fairfield church that Dave attended, that Banks Sturges had written the Queen about a family estate in England but that the inheritance had been in the courts so long it finally had reverted to the Crown.

The brush with New England culture did little to dull David Sturges' feeling for the mountains. On his return, he was right back at hunting and trapping and his duties as a guide.

One warm day in late spring, while the family was living at their Lewey Lake cabin, Charity Squires Sturges placed the infant Almira on a blanket in the health-giving sunshine of the grove outside the cabin door. The child remained there for some time, when weak but terrified sobbing indicated that something was wrong.

Dave Sturges, turned twenty, entered the clearing in time to see a hideous black panther standing over his sister's body, her small head almost within its strong jaws. There was no time for hesitation. Dave acted at once. Instantly, he aimed his rifle and fired. With a start, the voracious panther rolled over dead. Dave's skillful though dangerous shot had saved his baby sister's life.

Dave Sturges guided many parties of hunters throughout the years, and always did it well.

Verplanck Colvin, the State surveyor, recounted on January 8, 1870, to the members of the Albany Institute, a hunting trip with Sturges that began on Friday, December 31, 1869. He and Dave had started out on snowshoes after deer, when they came upon the trail of a large bear which, by every rule, should have been in hibernation at the time. For the remainder of the day, they followed the tracks without finding the animal. They returned to the Sturges House, where Dave lay on a couch, declaring that, trapper and hunter that he was, he had never been more tired. The trappers at the inn that night told Colvin and Sturges flatly that bear could not be successfully hunted in this way.

Nevertheless, the two were up before daylight on New Year's Day and out on the trail. By early afternoon the bear, a huge fellow of over 300 pounds, had been found and shot by Colvin.

"You have killed the biggest bear in Hamilton County!" Sturges told him. "Many New Yorkers whom I have guided, would have given a thousand dollars to have killed that bear."

David Sturges was truly one of Nature's noblemen. A kind, helpful person, he knew the woods thoroughly and could go anywhere in them. An outstanding man, he was a great fisherman and hunter. "Uncle Dave" was a favorite with all.

THE TIMES THEY TOOK A HOLT

WHEN ORIGINAL SETTLER Samuel Call's son, Lysander, grew to manhood at mid-century, he was one powerful fellow. Old Ben Gallup, who prized the young man's strength, liked to hire him to help with haying at the Gallup farm near Lake Pleasant's southeastern shore.

For a time, Lysander lived down at Burnham's Mills below the outlet of Lake Pleasant, working the sawmill and running the old up-and-down saws. Later, he built a house on the present site of Osborne's taproom near the lake's outlet. Finally, he moved to the Town of Benson, where he ran a fruit farm.

It was only after his death on January 3, 1918 that some of Lysander Call's physical feats began to come to light. On the subject of his ability as a fighter, Lysander never uttered a word.

Old Dan Cochrane did. The 250-pound Cochrane, himself a formidable fighter, was the son of a former English prize-fighter. Something of a local legend in his own right, Dan Cochrane ran a hotel at Wells. In his spare time, he served for years as county superintendent of schools.

Dan never could write. His vision, too, was badly impaired as the result of a blasting accident at Crandall's Bars when the highway was being constructed along the rocky promontory near the present State campsite below Wells. Dan's infirmities never really mattered. During inspections, Dan and Martha Cochrane would visit the schools together. Martha would do the inspecting while Dan sat silently by.

Dan Cochrane regarded Lysander Call much as he might a brother. And the approach of Lysander's son, Ed, caused reminiscences that would not down.

"Ed," asked Cochrane as he sat one day on the porch of his Wells hotel, "did Lysand ever tell you about the time we took a holt?" There was no time for Ed's reply. "We was both about an age, about twenty-one.

"The Fourth of July, we'd always go to the lake and have a ball game. After the game, we'd come down to Burr Sturges' sand beach for a swim.

"I says, 'Lysand, we never took a holt, did we? How'd you like to?'

" 'I don't care,' says Lysand. I never see a man but what I could take him by the shoulders, jack his knees and take him down.

"Well, we set to for a good long time, but not a thing happened. Neither one of us could get the other on his back."

Dan Cochrane smiled in satisfaction as he settled back in his vast, aged, porch chair.

Stories similar to those of Cochrane were also being circulated in the Town of Benson.

It all started, folks said, when George Swan opened a school of boxing on the floor of his old red barn. George had trained with such professionals as John L. Sullivan and knew how to handle himself well. When the semi-professional Swan completed his training, his students became the bullies of the countryside, challenging anyone who would dare to take them on. Call's reputation as a local strongman made him the most logical of candidates.

Elections in the town took place at Charles Hunter's house at the top of East Stony Creek Hill. They were all-day affairs, highly convivial in nature, with a bountiful dinner served at noon.

As the annual voting session approached, Lysander received word from the rambunctious George Swan.

"Bring your team and we'll knock the stuffin' out of you, and you can put it back in the wagon and take it back to the farm," was the relayed message.

Lystander agreed to attend the election, while promising that no team would be required.

On the day of the official function, the townsmen gathered

at the Hunter house in usual custom. Lysander had barely entered the doorway when Swan and his followers were ready for battle.

"Let's wait until after dinner and I'll have more to knock out," Lysander advised them impassively. Reluctantly, the would-be prize-fighters gave pause.

Dinner concluded, the political contests were momentarily forgotten as the townspeople gathered in a wide circle on the farmhouse lawn. Apprehension was registered among them when the measures of Swan's burly champions were taken.

As fitting instruction for his students, the semi-professional boxer decided to lead off with a demonstration. Warily, the two huskies entered the ring. George and Lysander sparred for some minutes in the improvised arena. Swan made out none too well.

Nevertheless, the able boxer was not to be defeated. For the next contest, he had two bystanders hold a wagon-tongue between himself and his adversary. The winner was to be the first to draw blood. Again, Swan and Call joined in vicious battle. In relatively short order, the challenger was put out of the contest with a smart crack of Lysander's fist to his nose.

As the warm afternoon sun moved toward the peaks of the western mountains, the battles continued. One after the other, the newly-trained prize-fighters were brought to the ring. It was ruled that each of the fighters would strike lightly. With the first drop of blood, the specific encounter was closed. One by one, the challengers were defeated at the powerful hands of Lysander Call.

It was Oscar Sweet, with his full 190 pounds, who was saved for the finale. When his time arrived, Oscar turned to his opponent's corner.

"Lysander, I won't lie to you," he boasted loudly. "I like to strike hard and I'll give you the same privilege."

"You're the first square, decent man I've met today," replied Lysander Call.

For a few moments, the two sparred menacingly. Suddenly, Lysander lunged with a smacking left full front.

Sweet clutched his face and started to lurch from the ring. "You've broken my jaw!" he shouted in pain.

Lysander had done just that. There is reason to believe that, during his lifetime, similar damage was done to other braggarts' bodies.

But Lysander Call never mentioned he'd had a holt of any-one—not to his dying day.

HERMITS OF LONG LAKE

NONE OF THE FOLKS at Long Lake will hazard whether the town drives people to the wilderness or the wilderness brings recluses to the town. They only agree that Long Lake has been long on hermits since even before the local government was formed.

Solitary living came into fashion in Hamilton County's northernmost district in 1830, when the hunter David Smith took to living on the shore of the lake that was for many years to bear his name. His retreat was an unfrequented, pathless forest in those early days.

Abiding grief was said to have sent David Smith to his wilderness setting. Shortly after his marriage, the wife whom he so dearly loved had died. He was a brooding type of person who sought solitude as his solace.

He had settled first, in the year 1820, at Stillwater over Inlet way, building a small, rude shanty which long afterward became the hermitage of Jimmy O'Kane. For ten years, he lived his lonesome life while hunting and trapping. As the location became more and more frequented by hunting and fishing parties, he went far up the river to the lake that was long to remain his home.

Here he made a little clearing, building a rough log shanty and raising potatoes in a small garden. Hunting and fishing were his passion and a primitive museum was acquired by his stuffing the skins of the animals and birds he killed. Summertimes, he would often take his little collection into the small growing settlements for exhibition.

But the principal attraction was Smith himself. Dressed in skins with the fur showing, his appearance was as wild as the animals he displayed.

During the extreme cold of winter, when game was scarce and deep snow covered the mountains, he sometimes suffered for lack of provisions. Once a bone from the moose meat he was eating lodged in his throat and he was unable to swallow. He almost died of hunger before he was able to make his way down to Fourth Lake for help.

Hermit or not, there was a brief period when David Smith saw fit to forego some of his much-touted privacy. At the first town meeting, when on April 3, 1838 the Town of Long Lake was formed, he was elected one of three highway commissioners. The following year, he was named an assessor and inspector of the two common schools of the town.

On July 2, 1840, the town board received peremptory notice: "I, David Smith do hearby apply to highway commissioners to lay and open a public and privit Road for my good and the good of town of Long Lake and the country in general, commenceing at the Lake betwene J. Plumley and D. Keller. Direction it this Day runing westerly to the house of David Smith in west part of the town of Long Lake. Distance betwene ten and twenty miles thru the woods in the best order shuning swamps and all bad land, crosing the inlet of tupers Lake as near the Lake as may be best, runing to the house ociped by sd. Smith at frount."

Smith's startling request was much like asking for the sky. To this day, his request has never been fulfilled. Nor was Smith ever elected to public office again.

Maybe it was in disgust over such wanton disregard by his

fellow townsmen. Maybe it was the increasing number of hunters and fishermen who began to intrude at Smith Lake. Probably it was a combination of both. In any event, Dave Smith, after contentedly living unmolested in his virgin setting for fifteen years, disgustedly closed his cabin door and left the locality—for the far west, some say, in search of more congenial surroundings.

Soon, his little clearing became covered with small trees from the encrouching forest, and his lonely deserted cabin crumbled into ruins. Even the name of the lake that remained his commemoration was changed when Dr. Seward Webb acquired the surrounding land he called Ne-ha-sa-ne Park. Smith Lake was rechristened Lake Lila in honor of Mrs. Seward; it bears the name today.

The Town of Long Lake was not to remain without its backwoods dwellers. Shortly, it was able to boast not one new hermit, but two.

Love and the world itself was said to have outlawed Ebenezer Bowen, who came from Canada shortly after 1850 at the age of forty-eight to build a rough cabin on a pine ridge just west of the outlet of Long Lake. Bowen was a gentleman of culture and refinement whose humble home was kept well supplied with fine books.

Unlike Smith, he never seemed to object to visitors, whom he greeted cordially and engaged in conversation. At intervals, he employed himself at charcoal-burning, piling wood in pyramid style, covering it with earth, and encouraging it to burn slowly for several days. It was the only labor he was ever known to perform.

The ambitious Robert Shaw of Long Lake Village, leader of the local Methodist church, used to visit Bowen occasionally to urge him into the fold. Never quite successful, Shaw promised the learned hermit he would surely seek the solace of religion before death came.

At last, as Bowen lay in his final illness, he sent a call for the expectant churchman. To Shaw's dismay, the hermit told him he knew he was about to die but had not changed his mind in the least. Ebenezer Bowen passed away in 1888 in his 86th year. A small marker in the Long Lake Cemetery signifies the location of his remains.

Long Lake accepted its two recluses with fitting dignity, listing them, incorrectly, to be sure, in its 1880 census. Ebenezer Bourne is the name given to Bowen by M. W. Lawrence, the enumerator from Lake Pleasant. Loring Trennier, age 45, is the official designation of the other. As for occupations—hermits, of course.

The man who called himself Laramie Harney followed Bowen from Canada in the early 1860's. Thirty-three years younger than his predecessor, he was born about 1835. Like Bowen, he was of the gentleman class of solitude seekers, refined in manner, dignified in bearing, but without Bowen's education. Settling in a miserable shanty at the northeast end of the lake on land belonging to Henry S. Harper, he engaged in farming. He kept cows, selling the milk to the early summer residents, and he raised and sold hay and kept a vegetable garden.

The blue-eyed Harney was a friendly person who enjoyed the companionship of others. Only in winters was his seclusion complete.

In his earliest days of Long Lake living, his dress was immaculate. Gradually, he permitted himself to become careless and unkempt.

Harney remained at Long Lake for some forty years. But in 1898, at the age of sixty-three, he became worried over a continuing illness. A friendly neighbor was sought to write a letter to the priest of the Canadian parish he had left, to inquire if any of his family still lived in the locality. For the first time in years, his real name was given, in confidence, to be sure. Residents recalled it as Laramie Fournier.

Months passed without answer. Then, in 1900, a son appeared to remove his aged and mysterious father. Nothing more was ever heard of him.

Long Lake would never be Long Lake without its resident recluse. By 1914, another had arrived to live in one of the nation's wildest areas at nearby Cold River Flow, nineteen miles from the nearest neighbor. Noah John Rondeau was thirty-three years old when first he came to build his crude shelter in his remote Adirondack retreat. He has lived in the same for almost fifty years.

In 1945, the frail Noah snowshoed out of the woods to Saranac for supplies. The round-trip through snow piled five-feet deep took him four full days and his vitality was impaired as a result.

In 1947, the State Conservation Department decided to ask the hermit if he would consider coming out of the woods through the snows of mid-February to assist with its exhibit at the National Sportsmen's Show in New York. From a helicopter, Bill Petty, district forest ranger, parachuted a message to the old recluse. Noah immediately tramped his word of assent in the snow.

At an advanced age, the modern-day hermit still lives in his solitary retreat, with occasional sportsmen his only visitors except for the local forest ranger, his good friend. Sometimes, messages are sent to acquaintances in the neighboring villages; otherwise, he remains removed from the world.

Long Lake people look upon Rondeau with a certain satisfaction, convinced they would be rather lost without a resident hermit at hand.

MOFFITT'S BEACH

IN THE mid-1920's, when the State of New York was active in building new public campsites, a choice location was selected along the east side of Sacandaga Lake in the Town of Lake Pleasant. Here in a large arm of the lake was one of the finest sand beaches in the Adirondacks. The view to the fore was superb. Back of the beach, the land rose steadily toward the public road. This was Moffitt's Beach.

The campsite proved a happy decision. The lovely, lake-side location has made it one of the finest of public recreation areas. Its ready and continuously growing popularity has caused its consistent enlargement until it is now the biggest public camp-site in New York State. Despite its regular and rapid develop-ment, Moffitt's Beach Campsite still cannot accommodate all who would use its considerable area and extensive facilities.

Through it, the name of Moffitt has become widely known by large numbers of vacationers in the eastern United States. Here they can come with tent and equipment to enjoy the ulti-mate in outdoor living. Here they find delightful picnicking grounds. Excellent swimming is at hand.

Lonely, aged Josiah Moffitt would have been surprised and proud to have realized that his dwindling family's name was to have been so perpetuated. Theirs was a sober history.

Josiah Moffitt, born in Massachusetts in 1802, had come to Lake Pleasant in 1835 with his wife, Mary, a native of New Jersey, from the Town of Glenville, Schenectady, N.Y. Ini-tially buying 200 acres of land in Lot 128 of the Moose River Tract west of Lake Pleasant Village, they ultimately settled on land on the eastern shore of then Round Lake. Here, on the outlet of adjoining Echo Lake, Josiah Moffitt built a mill for the manufacture of wooden bowls and novelty items.

An excellent mason and carpenter, Moffitt helped construct the old part of Hamilton County jail in 1839, as well as doing carpenter work on the old wooden courthouse in 1840. Mean-time, the industrious Mary Moffitt, who suffered from an ulcer, was said to have cleared the entire vlaie back of the beach.

Tragedy struck the family early. Mary Moffitt and two of their sons died of sunstroke on Moffitt's Beach one summer in the years between 1850 and 1860. They are buried in the little family graveyard, still discernible across the road from the campsite grounds. For a time, Josiah and his remaining son, Charles, lived on their land alone.

On November 7, 1861, Charles D. Moffitt, aged sixteen, enlisted in Company D, 93rd Regiment of New York Volunteers, destined for Civil War service. After three months, he died in a Washington hospital of fever.

Josiah Moffitt, the last of his family of six, was left alone. He remained in the area throughout the 1860's and became a member of the newly-formed Bible Class of Newton's Corners in 1867. Later, a lone and sorrowful man, he departed from the area, never to return.

On any mid-summer day in present years, Moffitt's Beach is anything but lonely. Josiah Moffitt would be pleased.

ON CALL

THERE WAS A TIME when you couldn't fire a gun anywhere around the corners at Lake Pleasant Village without hitting a Call. Not that anyone ever tried. The Calls were too valuable citizens to be spared. They were always the best of woodsmen, too, and chances were good you would get a dead-center gun shot in return.

The ample members of the family were everywhere. Walk into the local country store and a Call would appear to carve the cheese and weigh out the flour. Go to the hilltop hotel overlooking both Lake Pleasant and Round Lake and a Call would welcome you at the door. Enter the little county clerk's office next to the court house and find a Call in charge. It went on that way for years.

It all started when the educated Samuel Call came from New Lebanon, Connecticut, as a man of twenty-one, to the mountain county seat. Sam had detoured by way of Vermont and New York State's Fulton County. When he landed at Lake Pleasant in 1820, he jumped into community affairs with both feet.

Recognizing a good man when they saw one, Lake Pleasant folks chose him school commissioner, justice of the peace, and overseer of Road District Three, almost before he had time to hang up his battered broad-brimmed hat. And when Hamilton County got around to electing its own officers, Sam Call became the first county clerk.

Sam was elected clerk of the Town of Lake Pleasant in 1842. He would have taken the 1845 census of the town, too, if he hadn't had the confounded luck to break his leg so that Harvey Parkes had to serve in his place.

All of this would have proved sufficient to keep most men fully occupied from early morning until late at night. Somehow, Sam found time in the mid-1850's to take over operation of Hannah Pratt's grocery, known as the "Red Store."

Sam married Sally Abrams at Lake Pleasant on November 11, 1821. Together, they raised a family of five girls and four boys. As such, they started a rolling stone that plummeted right down through the better part of two centuries and into the present day. There's never been moss on any of the fast-moving Calls.

Funny thing about the Calls. They not only kept the village moving. They actually appear to have moved the village itself. Started down the road near the outlet, the village lost much of its activity to the hillside location up the road after the county buildings were constructed. Before the Calls had finished, they seem to have moved the general store and hotel, representing the full business section, right up there, too.

Sam Call's second son, Samuel R., was working at John C. Holmes' Lake Pleasant House, when word came that two men were arriving on a fishing expedition. Assigned to meet the guests at the railroad station fifty-four miles down the mountain roads in Amsterdam, Samuel R. harnessed up the buckboard and invited his younger brother, Lysander, to ride along.

When the soot-laden travellers alighted from the wheezing, puffing train, a third man, complete with baggage, was in the group. There was no room for Lysand.

"No worry," the husky younger Call told his brother, "I'll hike it back to the lake."

The old horse-drawn taxi started up the long hilly road, stopping at Fish House to feed horses and men. At night, the tired old nags drew to a halt before the mountain hotel. To the amazement of all, Lysander sat calmly waiting on the hotel porch, ready to help unload the trunks. His own foot power had beaten the horses to the lake.

Samuel R.'s experiences at the Lake Pleasant House qualified him to take over the older inn down at the outlet. Official sanction was granted in 1858 with a license to "keep an inn, tavern or hotel and sell strong and spirituous liquors." Some two years later, he was summoned to other pursuits out of the county, and his brother, Silas, took over the hotel.

When Civil War came, a fourth brother, Dave Abrams Call, was first in the town to go. The blond, blue-eyed Dave, age twenty-two, left his job as clerk in his father's store to enlist in April, 1861 and served for two years in Company C, 32nd Regiment. His older brother, Silas, served as county treasurer during the conflict and had the job of issuing bounties to the Hamilton County boys who went to war. An old unverified story tells that inspectors came to examine the county's books about that time and struck a difficult task. Sil had managed to lose a goodly number of his records at the bottom of the lake.

For some years, Silas Call ran the older hotel of the community. Then in 1880, he built a large and commodious establishment at the beautiful hilltop location back of the court house. First named Kun-ja-Muck Inn, general usage gave it the name of Call's Hotel. Broad piazzas lined the front and large, well-furnished rooms accommodated seventy-five guests. Later, under the proprietorship of J. Thomas Stearns, it became the Sacandaga Lake Hotel, which was burned in 1904 and was rebuilt in 1907 by J. D. Morley. When it burned once more in 1916, it was again rebuilt as the Hamilton Inn.

Like the others of his family from earliest times to the present, Sil Call was an outstanding woodsman. Lake Pleasant peo-

Lobb, the Fisherman. Lived for years as a hermit at Piseco Lake.

Benajah Page. The character and dignity of the mountain man is reflected in his bearing.

Biggest Load of Logs, drawn in 1915 on Sacandaga Lake by Selah Page of Speculator.

Bidwell's Hotel, landmark near Speculator, used as protection in a blizzard by the mail driver around 1874.

ple credit him with killing the last panther in the Adirondacks around mid-century, but argue whether his companion in such zoological extinction was Henry Courtney or Lysander Call. Those who champion the latter version say it happened on a ledge on the second hill up Robb's Creek from the main road. The dead panther was mounted and stood for years in the lobby of an Amsterdam hotel.

The original Samuel Call went and got himself buried in the cemetery on the south side of the lake in June, 1869, and there sat his general store. Lysander took over as storekeeper until the work got too confining for such a hardy man. The business was soon in the hands of younger brother, Dave. It was presumably Dave who moved the store from the outlet to the corners. Dave's son, Edgar, clerked in the store for many years taking over after his father's death in 1900. He remained the storekeeper until his death in 1922, when his widow, Margaret, ran the business. At her death in 1936, it was purchased by George Fuller and Kathleen Brooks, ending a proud history of eighty years of continuous store operation by the Calls.

But if the original Dave Call's branch of the family came to a halt at Lake Pleasant with Storekeeper Edgar's death, there was another Dave to carry on. The fifth of Silas Call's seven children, Dave married Burr and Sarah Thompson Sturges' daughter, Kitty, and lived for years in the community as farmer and guide. Among his wide accomplishments, Dave probably knew swearing better than any of his neighbors.

One day he drove his wagon up to Ernie Brooks' Hotel and went into the barroom for a drink. When he left, it was to find that one of his horses had dropped dead.

Dave had some round curses for inconsiderate animals, as preparations were made to remove the deceased. There was a final torrent of uttered violence.

"By jingo, I can buy 'em as fast as they can kill 'em off!" he declared.

Dave's sons, James "Burr" and Allen Douglas carried on in the family tradition. Educated for the teaching profession,

Doug's first job was at the old school in Gilmantown. After it was over, the young teacher affirmed that he didn't know how much the scholars had learned from books, but one thing sure, they certainly learned to play a good game of cards.

A gambler at times, Doug always seemed to lose. When he was with Battery C, 59th Field Artillery in World War I, he managed to save a hundred dollars.

"Might as well run it up to two hundred," said the enthusiastic soldier, as he entered an army game of poker. He got cleaned right out of funds.

Back at Lake Pleasant, he used to like to join the games that frequently took place at the Speculator House or the Brooks Hotel. On one such occasion, he got down to his last five dollars and left in dejection. Outside, Doug met a friend and offered him half of any money the friend could win, using his five dollars to start. The friend went into the game, but Doug simply could not stay away. Returning to the table, he placed his friend in the position of winning Doug's own money from the losing player and from the other players as well. He still came out ahead.

Doug's natural friendliness and engaging sense of humor made him a popular fellow. He early became supervisor of the town and was at the court house for forty years as deputy county clerk. He knew everyone and was known by all, permanent and summer residents alike. When he died on Christmas Day of 1960, the spot he had carved in the community virtually proved impossible to fill.

Doug did not go without leaving sons to carry on. Today, his son, Dave, is to be found at his Mobil service station at the four corners in Speculator, while his brother, Doug, Jr., holds forth on the hill overlooking the village.

Young Doug climbed Page Hill by a circuitous route to return to the hotel-keeping business his great-grandfather had begun. Eleven years before he was born, Marie R. Van Hoose of New York City had come to Lake Pleasant and stood atop the glorious hill. Before her down the steep mountain road, the picturesque, white-painted buildings of Speculator hugged the soft blue of the lake. Beyond, green-forested Speculator Mountain reared itself to proudest height. To the right, tranquil Sacandaga Lake glimmered above the treetops. Marie Van Hoose was entranced. Straightway, she purchased the property from Nathan R. Page. In this unusually beautiful setting, she built a lodge where, as singer and musician, she brought budding bards from the metropolis for instruction and living out of doors.

Local workmen were not always enthusiastic over the singing.

"I was painting outside a window," says one, "and thought it was the darnedest screeching I ever heard."

Marie Van Hoose died in Houston on April 17, 1916, leaving the property to her husband. After some years of intervening ownership, it was acquired by Hamilton and Frances Dunham Chequer, who opened the establishment as restaurant and inn. Through their efforts, the business grew, and several enlargements were made until it became one of the foremost inns in the locality.

When in 1960, the Chequers sold "Melody Lodge," with its full Adirondack flavor and breath-taking view, the new proprietors became none other than Doug and Dorothy Sohn Call, returning to keep a family tradition alive. Doug had been operating a large garage in New Jersey, but the memories of the mountains became an irresistible lure.

Local people were glad to have another Call back in the community. Old-timers say it sounds exactly like old times.

THE SELF-RELIANCE OF
FRENCH LOUIE

THERE WAS hardly a person in the entire Adirondacks who had not heard of Louie Seymour by the time the past century merged with the present. Everyone had his own stories about the famed old hermit. Each had his opinions of the unusual man. But on one point, all were agreed: The legendary French Louie was one of the few men in recent history who could exist in complete self-sufficiency, immune to the beneficences of modern civilization, add to its evils as well.

Louie was unable to make out entirely on his own when first he settled in the wilderness between Newton's Corners and Indian Lake. The first year, he would come striding into Ike Kenwell's lumber camp in the Cedar Lake section, seeking flour, pork and tea for his own use and grain for his chickens.

He always paid his debt. Toward spring, the hermit would return to the camp with a full bushel of fresh eggs. Asked his price by the always hungry lumbermen, Louie would reply, "No money for pork, no money for flour, no money for eggs."

After that, the French Canadian became more and more independent as he learned to fend for himself. His own food came largely from the fruits of his hunting and fishing. His chickens were fattened on fish and animal flesh.

Louie's route to his first little enclosed camp at Lewey Lake was circuitous. The overly zealous sternness of an unfeeling stepmother caused him to run away from his home at the community of Dog River, north of Ottawa. He was about twelve years old at the time, although he never did know his exact age. For twenty years, he worked on the Erie Canal or with small circuses in summers and as a lumberjack in winters. One day, near the end of the circus season in 1868, some lumberjacks spoke highly of the great wooded country around Indian Lake.

When ultimately he reached Indian Lake Village, Louie felt right at home with what he found. For some time, he worked for George Griffin, the lumberman, and later for others. But his real ambition was realized when, in 1873, he built his first cabin at Lewey Lake. Here he lived and trapped, selling his furs in the neighboring settlements of Newton's Corners or Indian Lake.

Although not a tall man, Louie was powerfully strong and completely fearless, a person whom few dared cross. Nor did most people want to provoke his mercurial anger. For Louie was a fellow whom most people liked at once.

It was not long before Louie's home became a shack made by Chet Sturges and Marinus Lawrence on West Lake. He worked on the place with the greatest of ambition. In two years, he had not only a livable mountain house, but a garden where good vegetables grew.

Louie's diet consisted of the fish he caught and the flesh of the venison and bear he shot, together with an occasional partridge or duck. This was supplemented with the produce of his garden and with flour and meal brought back from the settlement. Sweetening he obtained by tapping maple trees and collecting sap in white birch-bark buckets of his own making. From the sap, he made his maple syrup and maple sugar.

He kept chickens for fresh eggs. He also owned two hound dogs. When he went into town, to be gone a week, he would kill a deer, skin it, and leave it, along with a pail of water, for his dogs that were left chained back at his camp. He would also fill a trough full of water and leave ample corn for his chickens. The animals and fowls always made out well.

Bear grease and deer tallow were his shortening. The Lawrence hunting camp is on the ground where Louie lived at Pillsbury Lake. Some years after Louie had gone, one of Sam and Elizabeth Satterlee Lawrence's children found a hard, black object. When cut into, it proved to be a white piece of tallow that had withstood many seasons.

Louie attributed the success of his garden to the snakes of

the area, which he made his pets. They killed his potato bugs, he said. No one was allowed to harm his snakes and Louie saw that they were carefully nourished and provided with nesting places of his own design. A couple of knocks on the meat block and the snakes would come gliding out to be fed.

The hermit fertilized his garden well by planting fish with his seed. Later, he made his own type of compost hole with the discarded entrails of the animals he caught near his cabin.

One winter Sunday, Ed Brooks went over to Louie's camp to catch some trout in West Canada Lake. Louie told him the fish were not biting, although Ed found numerous holes in the ice. Unsuccessful in his fishing, Ed went back to Louie's camp that afternoon. Louie promptly threw open the door of an unused room, sixteen feet wide, at the end of his cabin. Frozen trout were piled breast high inside.

"Help yourself," the hermit invited him. Spring was approaching and the uneaten store would soon be tossed in his pit for use as fertilizer.

Jim Sturges was once in the area when Louie was dressing his garden. The decayed fish and venison were being exhumed and Jim said they could be smelled for a mile.

Arriving at Louie's under similar circumstances, Harry Wilber and Kenneth Sturges found the decayed flesh running and the stench overpowering. Harry was not only nauseated by the smell, but his senses were additionally outraged when he saw some twenty large snakes sunning on Louie's stone pile.

Proof of the effectiveness of the method was always found in Louie's rhubarb. Those who saw the stalks told that they would reach over the top of a pack basket and were as thick as your arm.

Harry and Ken had dug worms for fishing on the Miami River and had put them in a sack to keep them cool. They were some miles into the forest before they remembered that the bait had been left behind. In the emergency, Louie was consulted. The old hermit went to a bed of soft earth and forked over the soil. The men's eyes popped when huge night-crawlers began to emerge.

"You can't have them," cautioned Louie, to their immense surprise. "They not ripe yet. They must be white."

Louie's habits of cleanliness were scarcely beyond reproach. Marinus Lawrence would often go trapping with the hermit and remain all winter. The first time, Louie killed and dressed a deer. He was bloody to his elbows when he started to prepare the evening meal.

"Aren't you going to wash?" Rene Lawrence asked him.

"Once you start trapping, you don't wash," Louie instructed. "It kills human scent."

"Well, Louie, you do your cooking, and I'll do mine," was Rene's reply.

"All right," said Louie, as he picked up a dirty sock and wiped the grease from his frying pan.

Al Sturges was with Louie one winter and they ate nine deer. Louie would warm the deer flesh for ease in removing the hide, then chop up the meat. In one continuous process, he would start cooking the stew, skimming off the deer excrement that appeared regularly on the surface of the boiling water.

Ed Brooks' squeamishness about the untidiness of the old hermit's household caused Louie to name him "tenderfoot." Ernie Brooks, the lumberman and inn-keeper, and his brother were cruising timber on West Canada one day when Ernie suggested they stop in on Louie for a bite to eat.

"What'll you have, Brooks?" Louie asked Ernie, and the luncheon menu was concluded with little ado.

Ed was less easily satisfied.

"You can boil me a couple of eggs," he said. "At least they ought to be clean."

Louie was happy to oblige. He did not resent Ed's opinion a bit.

Louie became a much sought-after guide for parties of sportsmen. He enjoyed working with them and did everything possible for their comfort. He kept lean-tos at various mountain locations on land he never owned, and never objected to their use by others. His clothing was almost always supplemented by contributions from the hunters, while a rope around his waist served as a belt.

At the conclusion of one of Louie's visits to town, he was to join with a Gloversville clergyman and his party to serve as guide. They found Louie unusually quiet at the end of a customary spree and not feeling overly well.

"Louie," said the clergyman back at camp, "I don't know what I'm going to do with you if you don't behave better. I guess I'll have to string you up and clean out your inwards like that deer over there."

There was no response. Conversation remained at lowest ebb.

The next day, the two were carrying a canoe to the lake shore, the clergyman at the bow and Louie lugging the stern. Quietly, Louie spoke.

"Parson," he said sonorously. "You leave my guts alone."

Like most men of the mountains, Louie never had much use for the State Conservation Laws. He told one game warden, who hid out and watched him for the greater part of a day, that he had known of his proximity through two or three signs. He quietly warned the official that he looked like a deer to Louie when he was seen in the woods.

Ernie Brooks and French Louie were once feeding oats to a deer at a skidway over on Mud Lake. Louie looked longingly at the fine specimen of forest game while remembering the wild partridge that Ernie had shot that day. As was his custom, Louie began muttering to himself.

"By quipes, Brooks killed my tame partridge. I'll kill his tame deer."

Ernie smiled to himself at Louie's distortion of the truth. It was the hermit's own rationalization for intended action.

Freedom was Louie's watchword and he never yielded to the world's routine.

An Amsterdam man, suffering from tuberculosis, went with

a companion to Louie's camp at West Canada to spend the winter in an attempt to improve his health. Unpacking their duffel bags while Louie was out of the cabin, one man drew out a calendar and hung it on the wall.

It was the first thing that met the hermit's eyes when he reached the door. Instantly, he snatched the offensive decoration from the wall and shoved it into the stove.

"If you stay with me, tomorrow will be just like today, and today just like yesterday—no different," he pronounced.

He had small need for clocks or watches, either. Sometimes he carried an alarm clock wrapped in a blanket in his pack basket. More often, he used no time-piece at all.

Isaiah Perkins, searching for a horse that had wandered into the woods, sought Louie's help at West Canada Lake. As they walked the trail, Isaiah noticed that he had neglected to wind his watch.

"Louie, got any idea what time it is?" he asked.

"Remember that bird I spoke to you about?" answered Louie. "That was about a mile back, about fifteen minutes. That's what I call '5 o'clock bird.' It 5:15 now."

Isaiah set his watch and checked the time when he returned to town. It was not more than five minutes off.

As he grew older and the occasional pains of advanced years plagued his muscle-hardened body, Louie decided that the time had arrived to prepare for the death that must inevitably come. He dug his own grave. In times of illness, he would stay in this grave, covering it with an improvised shelter, until he was well enough to return to his cabin. He had great physical endurance and, even at an elderly age, he was able to undergo tests of strength that would have sent most younger men to defeat.

A sportsman from New York City once found Louie searching diligently back of his camp at Pillsbury. Inquiry revealed he had misplaced a baking powder can containing some .30-.30 "cattridges" and forty dollars in bills.

Together, the two searched, the visitor commiserating over the monetary loss.

"Never mind the forty dollars," Louie told him. "It's the cattridges I want."

"Where I come from," said the sportsman in the retelling, "money is important, but not to him."

The remark summarized the man for whom civilization had so little importance. One could laugh at his habits, deplore his faults. Yet Louie was in every sense a model woodsman, whose deep-seated self-reliance could only win admiration and respect.

WHEN LOUIE WENT TO TOWN

WHEN FRENCH LOUIE settled on the life of a hermit, his renunciation of civilization was as complete as it could possibly become. It was not without several trials to prove that backwoods living was his unmistakable choice.

Any question of his returning to Canada had been early answered in the negative. Years before, he had gone quietly back to his home and had stood at the barn, watching his younger brothers and sisters at play. He had learned that his father and stepmother had separated. Somberly, he had turned away. No one ever knew he had been there.

Louie once left the mountains to join a small circus that had come to town. When the show went into winter quarters, Louie found himself in Maine. In early spring, he left with the law in hot pursuit. He had shot a deer out of season. His pursuers were eluded when, coming to a log-filled stream, he hopped aboard and rode the logs to safety.

Back in the Adirondacks, he built himself a rough camp up the Indian Lake road near Fish Hatchery Brook. Shortly afterward, he took a job cleaning some of Dave Sturges' land and stayed for a time at the Sturges House. He also lived for a period down East Road with Olive Arnold, after she had separated from her husband. But he soon left. This was the way of life he wanted to escape.

Thereafter, Louie's contacts with the outside world were only when local hunters or city sportsmen found their way to his cabins, or during his twice-yearly visits to Newton's Corners to sell furs. The principal expedition was made in March, the old hermit lugging his winter's take on a long, narrow handsleigh of his own making. At such times, he would bring 150 deerskins and enough of the pelts of fox, mink, marten and 'coon to net him five to six hundred dollars or more in one fell swoop.

Arriving at the top of Page Hill, overlooking the village, he would emit a series of piercing, wild-animal cries that would bring the school kids running. Louie never failed to buy them candy or distribute nickels and dimes. Always the youngsters would beg him to mimic an owl or a wild forest animal; always he would oblige. He liked children, but seldom had much use for grown-ups.

When he had reached the Brooks Hotel, the old hermit would fill his mouth with tobacco and call for the first of an interminable series of drinks of "whickey." After a few weeks of generous spree, his money exhausted, he would shoulder his pack basket and lumber heavily up Page Hill empty-handed, except perhaps for a piece or two of salt pork. Often he spent as much as nine hundred dollars on his sprees.

People said that he would spend every cent he made from his previous six months of hunting and trapping. But Louie had a secret shared only with John F. Buyce, the blacksmith and boat builder. Before beginning his serious drinking, the old hermit would hand John F. a sum of money for safe-keeping. There was sometimes as much as $500 in the old blacksmith-shop safe waiting for Louie's use.

During his early spring visits, Louie would wade through the mud and melting snow three to four inches deep from the Brooks Hotel to the Speculator House and back. He liked to favor both with his patronage.

"Aren't your feet cold?" the ever-present children would ask.

"No," Louie would reply, "I wear good home-knit wool socks. No matter how wet they get, they're always warm and dry." He wore the socks summer and winter.

The old French Canadian was hardly the most unobjectionable of hotel guests. Wallowing through the deep mire of the village thoroughfare, he would head for his room and go to bed without removing an article of clothing.

Occasional illnesses from his drinking were not unknown, and use of his boot as a chamber pot was fairly routine. His drunkenness was sometimes a problem. And the loud animal calls he gave at almost any hour of day or night were startling, to say the least.

Once he almost started a riot at the bar of Osborne's Adirondack House when he accused the St. Regis Indian, Johnny Leaf, of stealing traps. Johnny drew his knife and went for him. Louie knocked the Indian down and punctuated his action by throwing a big, brown cuspidor at Johnny's head, spattering the tobacco juice all over the Indian's face. Bystanders quickly ushered Leaf out the door before things really got rough.

Hotel keepers championed his substantial trade, but breathed a sigh when he was seen to shoulder his pack and trudge slowly up Page Hill.

The story is told by Harvey L. Dunham in his book, *French Louie,** that on one of his return trips to camp he had salt pork in his pack. "He was quite unsteady, when, just before climbing Blue Ridge, he settled down on some matted grass in the sun. It was a good spot to rest and sleep it off. The spring air was quiet and warm and Louie lay for a long time. When he reached around to adjust his shoulder straps, he thought he had lost his pack. The hedgehogs had eaten up all of his salt pork and even a good part of the basket! They had eaten it right off his back."

* Harvey L. Dunham. *Adirondack French Louie*. Utica, N.Y. 1952.

In later years, one or more of the men from the village would return with Louie to his camp to insure that he made it safely home. Sam Lawrence went with him as a boy.

"By quipe," said Louie as they hiked up the road, "the nest will be full of eggs."

Sam found them virtually overflowing.

At Louie's invitation, young Bill and Bob Osborne once accompanied him back to his camp. The boys preceded him across the muddy Miami River flats. Louie was feeling none too well and walked slowly behind. After waiting for an interval, the two Osbornes back-tracked and found the hermit lying in the mud up to his whiskers.

"Flies bite," he told them.

The boys urged him to continue the trek.

"No farther," replied the hermit, "get feet all wet."

Louie told them where to find the keys to his cabin. The next morning, he came stalking into Pillsbury.

Ed Carpentier, the sometimes summer resident, borrowed J. Howard Hanson's lakeside summer camp for one of his recurring honeymoons. One day, Louie appeared at the door.

"By quipe," he said, laying a sizable box on the table, "I brought you something."

Thinking it was a mess of freshly caught fish, the recipients removed the cover. The new Mrs. Carpentier uttered a piercing shriek and almost fainted when out crawled a huge snake. With Louie's passion for snakes as pets, his gift could not have been a more well-meant sacrifice. He was generously giving something of himself.

Despite his gargantuan sprees in the village, Louie's firm rule was never to drink while in the woods. It was too dangerous for one who lived alone and must depend on his own resources at all times. When Dan Cochrane's son, Bill, ran the Speculator House, he and Bion Page went through snow as high as the branches of the trees to see if Louie was safe and well. Cochrane carried a bottle of whiskey as a present.

"I don't want it," protested Louie when the gift was made. "But leave it here. Maybe someone will come along and want a drink."

In the winter of 1915, French Louie became ill. A pain gnawed continuously in his side and he could barely get his breath. He decided a trip to the Corners was in order. His preparations consisted, in part, of catching four sizable trout through holes he had opened in the ice.

The following day, Louie donned his snowshoes and tramped through the zero air. That night, he stayed at his camp at Pillsbury. The next day, he was on the trail at dawn. When he reached the road, he removed his snowshoes and walked the remainder of the way to Speculator.

Arriving at Brooks Hotel, he first gave his trout to Nora Brooks, wife of the proprietor. Then he went to the bar.

In the evening, he was taken sick. Ernie and Nora Brooks gave him the best of care and a doctor was called. He died in the early hours of Saturday morning.

The townspeople pitched in to help. Ernie Brooks went to the town clerk's office for the burial permit and agreed to buy the coffin. R. H. Perry of Wells was hired as undertaker. Mead Sturges and Nathan Slack dug the grave.

The Town of Arietta helped, too, by agreeing to share the burial expenses with the Town of Lake Pleasant at a cost of $76.90 to each town.

The school was closed on Louie's funeral day. The young students sat in two front-row pews while the sermon was preached by the Rev. L. W. Ward. Before the casket was closed, the children filed by and laid fresh, green balsam sprays over Louie's body. In the procession to the cemetery, they held balsam boughs before them as they walked.

Louie was buried in the cemetery at Speculator. For years, the grave was unmarked. Now it is designated by a tombstone that reads: "French Louie"—Louis Seymour, died Feb. 28, 1915 aged about 85 years. Erected 1954 by admirers."

Louie's gun, given originally by him to Ernie Meyrowitz,

a summer resident, can now be seen at Camp-of-the-Woods.

The story of Louie Seymour has a way of coming into about every conversation about the mountains of yesteryear. Louie himself would not be surprised. He always said that, after he died, he would return. In a real sense, he was right.

DID LOUIE HAVE A HERMIT BROTHER?

ODDLY ENOUGH, a second hermit bearing the name of Seymour lived at Lewey Lake at the same time as French Louie. The two had much in common, though Sam Seymour lacked the flamboyancy of Louie.

Sam Seymour lived on Lewey Lake's opposite shore. Like Louie, he was French Canadian. Like Louie, he was a huntsman and trapper. Sam, however, was not one to go deeply into the mountains. He was good at making dugouts and had one at Lewey Lake and one at Dug Mountain.

Sam was built like Louie. Short and stocky, he had the same reddish-brown hair and blue-black eyes. They had seen each other often at the lake. Yet each had gone his way silently, refusing to be the first to speak.

Was it possible that they were brothers? Sam thought so. One day, at the general store at Indian Lake, he confronted Louie quietly.

After a solemn greeting, Sam remarked of the strangeness of the fact that both had the same last name. But Louie pointed out that there were many Seymours in Canada.

Sam persisted. It was odd, he felt, that both came from the same part of Canada. What is more, both hailed from Dog River.

Maybe it was funny, Sam said, but he felt that the two were brothers.

Louie thought for a moment. Surely, he had had enough brothers and sisters, but he did not remember a brother named Sam, he said.

Each told that their family had broken up in Canada and each related the same tale of a difficult stepmother.

They left the store together and started down the road to the south. For a while, they saw much more of each other. After a time, Sam induced Louie to live with him. But Sam differed from Louie in many respects. Sam did not drink. He liked people and welcomed newcomers openly. He was neat and clean. Louie required his sprees and paid little attention to anyone.

For about a month, they lived together. Then Louie moved back to his own cabin. He had trapper's work back in the mountains, he said. Sam remained alone.

Their careers were parallel in other respects. In 1905, at the age of seventy-two, Sam Seymour was a boarder in town working as a lumberman, but he soon returned to the life he loved at Lewey Lake.

The summer after Louie died, Sam was found ill and in distress at his cabin. Groceries were ordered sent by the town fathers, but soon it was apparent that Sam was too ill and too weak to care for himself. John F. Buyce was commissioned to take a team and bring him to the village. Walter Dunham was hired to go to his cabin and bring out his personal effects. Susan Parslow did his washing. He was brought for a time to the Lake Pleasant home of William Parslow. There, in early July, 1915, he died.

Ashley Perkins took an automobile to Lewey Lake to bring out anything of value that belonged to Sam. His "goods" were advertised in the local newspaper, published at that time by Vernon E. Dewey of Wells.

R. H. Perry of Wells was sought to provide the casket and undertaking services. Earl Parslow was hired to lay out the body, and George Sturges and Walter Page dug the grave. The

The Old Catholic Church at Morehouseville, abandoned and destroyed after its door was nailed shut in the 1860's.

Kreuzer's Hotel, Morehouseville. Built before 1880, it had become a popular resort around the turn of the century.

The Old Court House at Lake Pleasant, built in 1840 and replaced in 1929.

View of Lake Pleasant about 1900, from the hilltop where the ancient Indians held their council fires.

funeral sermon was preached by the Rev. L. W. Ward in the Methodist Church at Speculator.

His obituary in the Gloversville *Morning Herald* was succinct:

"Thursday, July 15, 1915—Samuel Seymour, who for the past few years has resided near Lewey Lake, died at the home of William Parslow, Friday afternoon. Mr. Seymour has lived in this section during the last thirty years, having passed most of the time in the woods in much the same manner as did Louis Seymour. Although no one seems to know his exact age, it is thought that he was about 85 years old. The services were held at the church Sunday at 2 P.M., the Rev. Ward officiating. Interment was in the village cemetery."

Sam's is an unmarked grave. No admirers have come forth to erect a tombstone. Rather, he lies in the solitude he always sought, yet with a wistful aspect when one remembers that he enjoyed the companionship of others and always welcomed people to his rude little home.

UNSOLVED MYSTERIES OF
HAMILTON COUNTY

"ANOTHER of the unsolved mysteries of Hamilton County" is a favorite newspaper expression when a seemingly inexplicable event has occurred. Hamilton County has them—a long series of enigmas, as inscrutable as the mountains and the woodlands themselves.

Such was the case of Perry Page, one of the best-known guides in the Southern Adirondacks.

Carved much in the mold of the mountain hermit, Perry was born in 1860, the oldest son of Benajah and Sarah Page, who lived at the summit of Page Hill. For years, Perry guided parties of sportsmen from the hotels of Lake Pleasant Village.

Then increasingly he took to the forests, at length building himself a camp across Sacandaga Lake on the shores of Mud Lake. Here he preferred to remain.

Perry would make occasional visits to his family home to spend the night while his mother was alive. After that, he was seen less frequently by the townspeople. In winters, he would leave his camp and no one knew where he was. Somewhere, deep in the snow-covered forests, he would be setting a line of traps.

Perry used to leave his camp occasionally to hike around Sacandaga Lake and get his supplies at Call's store at Lake Pleasant Village. On his way, he made a habit of stopping at Searing's on Fish Street to trade venison for homemade butter and bread.

Late one fall around 1925, after hunting season had closed, Perry left his camp and brought fresh venison to Mrs. Searing, who gave him the usual butter and bread and, this time, a cake as well. It was getting dark when he left for home and she invited him to stay.

Perry declined. He had left a pack basket full of venison on the trail and his gun against a tree. There was danger of the game protector discovering such unwarranted loot.

Perry enjoyed drinking occasionally, but Mrs. Searing noted that he had not been drinking at the time. She had helped him take the pack from his back and had observed that it contained no bottle.

Some time later, a local hunter was hiking in the area of Mud Lake, when he came upon Perry's pack basket. Moving on to the hermit's deserted cabin, he found Perry's mail and the groceries he had brought back from Lake Pleasant, including the delicacies given him by Mrs. Searing. There was a plug of tobacco with one small chew taken from the corner. His boots had been set by the stove.

Looking further, the huntsman found Perry's boat bottom-side up on the lake shore, with a mitten nearby.

A search was immediately conducted, without result. Later,

when the ice went out of the lake, the men of the town were on hand to watch. For weeks, they dragged the lake without reward.

Perry Page, age sixty-five, had simply vanished. His body has never been found.

There was the strange case, too, of Henry Streeter, brother-in-law of Henry Courtney. Streeter had gone to the Civil War and used to remark that, due to the clerical type of duty to which he had been assigned, he was never near a fired shot.

But if he had escaped the use of guns in the Army, it was not to leave them in home life, where hunting was as part of living. On October 31, 1875, Streeter went hunting with a group of neighboring men down the Elm Lake Road. As the day drew to a close, it became evident that Streeter was missing. His companions became uneasy.

Streeter kept a rowboat on Elm Lake and fears were expressed that he might have drowned. Quickly, a search was instigated.

To the horror of his companions, Henry Streeter's lifeless body was found in the woods no great distance away. Investigation showed a bullet hole through his forehead.

One member of the party was found with Streeter's gun. He had traded with Streeter earlier that day, he declared. Streeter had always carried his change in a small box in which caps for muzzle-loading rifles were packed. The same man had the cap box, too.

There were rumblings about these circumstances, but the man in question was of a well-known family. Although suspicion was general, no investigation was made. Henry Streeter had escaped war-time battle, only to die mysteriously by a bullet in the peaceful beauty of his own homeland.

It was somewhat like the case of William Blackwood Meveigh on August 27, 1896. The Meveighs were born in Belfast, Ireland. When they arrived at Lake Pleasant about 1878 to settle just west of the lake, their name was spelled McVeigh, as any good Irishman's should be. But they decided

it sounded more Irish than American, so by pure usage the
spelling was changed to Meveigh.

Bill Meveigh had an Irishman's capacity for liquor. So when,
returning from a trip to Wells that warm August evening, he
found driving his team difficult, he simply let the horses find
their own way. All went well until he reached Guide Board
Hill on the old Wells road.

It was Jim Higgins, coming later up the same road, who
found him. Meveigh's wagon was off the road and Bill had
fallen over the embankment. His head had hit a rock in his
tumble. Bill Meveigh was dead.

Had he been forced off the road by an unknown assailant?
The family wondered. No one was ever to know.

Unfathomable occurrences are not confined to the distant
past.

Mel Slack, the former guide who lived at Perkins Clearing,
was berrying in the vicinity in October, 1952, when he came
upon a black sedan half-hidden in the brush off the Speculator-
Indian Lake road. Mel noted that the automobile bore a Minnesota license when he reported his findings to the authorities of
the town.

Systematic investigation of the vehicle's contents was undertaken by Mel, Clyde Elliot and Ranger Halsey Page. They
found a man's pocketbook, without money, but with driver's
license and papers intact. A baby's cap and baby's toys were
scattered on the rear seat. A yellow telegram advised the re-
cipient that he was to report for work in Philadelphia ten days
previous.

Messages were immediately dispatched to Philadelphia and to
Minnesota. Yes, came the reply from the western state, the man
in question had been reported missing when he had failed to
return to his family. Little else was known.

Some days later, Game Protector Homer Preston was prob-
ing the best methods of planting fish in Mason Lake. There,
floating on the water's placid, reflective surface was the body

of a man. An autopsy was held and several versions were given. Travellers' checks and identification were found.

Why was the man fully six miles from his automobile? Why was he in this remote section at all? What about the scar on the back of his head that seemed to indicate he had received a heavy-handed blow? The answers have never been given.

It was another of the mysterious deaths in the imponderable mountains. No one knows the causes, nor the answers. Many feel that mountain mysteries are better left unsolved.

PREPARATIONS FOR THE HUNT

THE NIGHT before "Burr" Sturges and Oscar Howland were heading into Mason Lake on an extended hunting and fishing trip, Oscar came up from Wells to stay at Burr's house at Newton's Corners.

The next morning, the Wells resident offered to help speed preparations by going out to feed the oxen and yoke them to the wagon that was to carry the men's supplies. He was gone a long time. When he returned, Oscar was tired right out.

"Where've you been so long?" Burr Sturges wanted to know.

"Had an awful time," Oscar observed wearily. "Couldn't get those fool oxen into their durned yoke."

Burr Sturges paused in his feverish preparations long enough to peer out the window. What he saw caused him to gasp loud and long.

"What in tarnation you doing with my black heifer!" he roared.

Oscar had to admit that maybe he had made a mistake.

*   *   *   *   *

When Abe Lawrence, Orrin Griffith and Jim Sturges were preparing for a hunting trip deep into the mountains, it was left to Abe to stock in provisions.

Abe promptly sat down to make out his list. After diligent work, he unsmilingly handed the paper to the others for approval.

Orrin studied the list carefully. "Loaf of bread, bottle of whiskey," he read. "Loaf of bread, bottle of whiskey." The tally continued indefinitely in the identical vein.

Orrin faced Abe squarely with a pertinent question.

"What in hell you going to do with so much bread?"

UNCLE DAVE'S STURGES HOUSE

HOTEL BUSINESS always held a fascination for David Sturges. His duties as guide kept him in close contact with the hotels of the area, allowing him to observe the details of their operation, giving him confidence in dealing with their guests. He was especially familiar both with Clark Satterlee's small establishment at Newton's Corners and with John C. Holmes' Lake Pleasant Hotel. This, he decided, was for him.

John C. Holmes' daughter, Irene Matilda, the young schoolteacher whom Dave was courting, was equally interested. Dave thought he saw a likely location. His oldest brother, Aaron Burr Sturges, had married Sarah Thompson, daughter of John and Anna Dunham Thompson, whose family owned the land directly across the road from Clark Satterlee at Newton's Corners.

The Thompsons, who had moved to Wells, were perfectly agreeable that Dave build on a part of their land, but money was needed for lumber. Dave went down to Burnham's Mills, where William Burnham's son, Wallace, ran the sawmill, and took a job, working there until he had earned enough to buy the lumber for the inn he planned to build.

When at length the day arrived when Dave felt his finances were sufficiently secure, Wallace Burnham put an extra plank in the mill dam, causing the water slowly to rise. The lumber for Dave's hotel was thrown into the mill pond and rafted the two miles to the bridge over the outlet stream of Lake Pleasant. From there, it was hauled by wagon to Dave's selected location.

Burnham's method of water transportation, roundly applauded on this occasion, later fared less well. The lumberman was hauled into court by Alonzo Wilber when his extra plank in the dam threatened to become a permanent fixture and was raising the water level so markedly that it prevented use of the ford at the outlet of the lake.

The year 1858 was an important one for Dave Sturges. At the age of twenty-six, he married Irene Matilda Holmes. At the same time, the construction of his Sturges House was begun. For ten years, David and Irene Matilda worked to build their new business. On December 11, 1868, Irene M. Holmes Sturges died at the age of thirty-five.

It was a terrible loss to Dave, who could not possibly hope to carry on alone. He thought he had an answer. Susan Mahala Fountain had worked for years at the Lake Pleasant Hotel and was well-schooled in the business. She was his sister-in-law, in any case, through the marriage of Dave's sister, Sarah, to Mahala's brother, David Fountain. Perhaps she could be induced to take over the distaff side of his hotel business.

Mahala Fountain, two years older than Dave, agreed. For many years, they ran the famous hotel together. Near the turn of the century, Dave married Ida M. Weaver of Wells, who thereby became "land lady" at the hotel.

After Joel Newton's establishment was razed by fire, the Newton's Corners post office moved briefly to Toles Satterlee's store, then to the Sturges House. But Dave's easy-going ways caused him to be accused of carelessness in allowing liquor to be sold too close to the official premises. The post office was removed, and for several years, the residents of Newton's Corners were required to go to Lake Pleasant Village for their mail.

There were twenty-four "boarders" at the Sturges House in August of 1877, while Stephen D. Andrews' Lake Pleasant Hotel had only seven. That was the month when Dave was out on the lawn assisting several of his feminine guests at shooting target. Dave was watching to see who made the best score when a ball fired by a Mrs. Craig of Albany glanced off a tree, struck a second tree, then entered the hotel-keeper's body. Fear of hemorrhage prompted Dr. Thomas McGann and Dr. C. R. Blake to leave the ball within Dave's side. He carried it there throughout his life.

The Sturges House was in full swing when the summer visitors began to arrive in large numbers in the nineteenth century's final decade.

Located just above the village four corners, it was a long two-story white building with croquet ground on the grassy lawn to the front and tennis courts at the rear. The comfortable old lobby, lounge and dining rooms, with ample fireplaces, were well-supplied with the mounted heads of woodland animals killed over the years. The inevitable verandas were ample at front and side of the house. In later years, an annex building had been constructed across the dirt roadway in an unsuccessful effort to accommodate all who sought the hospitality of the well-known inn.

People came to spend week-ends or their all-too-brief summer vacations. Some families remained for the full eight-week season. Many returned year after year. Even after several of the city visitors had begun to build their own summer homes along the shores of the lake, they used the Sturges House as headquarters while opening their places in the spring and closing them in the fall.

Regular visitors to the Sturges House furnished their own rooms, keeping the same accommodations year after year. The other guests helped themselves to whatever they required from the unoccupied rooms.

The hotel's water supply was dipped from the lake near the outlet into barrels that stood on a big flat truck drawn by horses down the dirt road to the present public beach. Children of hotel guests could always get a ride to the lake, but never back.

Friday was always fish day at the Sturges House. Each Thursday, the wagon would leave the hotel for the lake shore with an ample supply of nets. In a few short hours, it would come lumbering back up the road with sufficient lake trout to feed from 150 to 200 guests the following day.

As Dave Sturges grew older, he had a croquet lawn made in the yard of his inn. Here he and T. L. Ostrander of Wells played very serious matches. Everyone could follow their progress. If Tom went home in the afternoon, the local saying was that "Dave dun up Tom today." If Ostrander defeated Dave, he would remain for the evening meal, driving away in his horse and buggy after 7 o'clock.

Dave took his croquet mighty seriously in those days. Nothing irritated him more than being called from an internecine contest for the more mundane duty of receiving arriving guests at the Sturges House.

"I wish the hotel was in hell!" he was often quoted as saying on such occasions.

"Uncle Dave" Sturges died September 15, 1920 at the age of eighty-eight, and management of the Sturges House passed to the Magee Family. During the second World War, it was destroyed by fire. The Sturges House annex remained to become a smaller inn known as Oak Mountain Lodge, operated by John and Genevieve Zieser, natives of Amsterdam, but the tradition both of Dave Sturges and his Sturges House remain as lasting and important parts of Lake Pleasant lore.

CAPTAIN PARKER'S RETURN

OVER AT Long Lake, where history has a habit of repeating itself, a new Captain Parker has been acquired. It happened when the boys of the Long Lake Volunteer Fire Department set out to organize an Emergency and Rescue Squad. Supervisor Arthur Parker, chairman of the county board of supervisors, was their choice to head the new organization. Art was elected captain, and just in time. Within two weeks, the squad was called deep into the woods on the Brandeth Tract for an errand of mercy.

Announcement of the name "Captain Parker" brought a jarring note to Long Lake people. Old timers remember well the white-bearded old man who lived among them for about sixty years. His renown has similarly been passed along to the younger folks. The original Captain Parker was a towering, lank, old character whose legend will long remain.

Despite the similarity of name, no blood relationship exists between the new Captain Parker and the old. There are several parallels, however.

The present Captain Parker descends from his great-grandfather, Zenas, one of the earliest settlers and first to be elected overseer of the poor and commissioner of schools at the initial town meeting on April 3, 1838. By 1847, Zenas had become supervisor, preceding his great-grandson in the office by some one hundred and twelve years. Captain Calvin S. Parker, for his part, arrived in the locality in 1858.

Both were New Englanders, Zenas coming from Vermont and Calvin from Massachusetts. Art's grandfather, Richard, who served in Company F, 192nd Regiment, during the Civil War, was Captain Calvin's younger contemporary. Captain Calvin was a sturdy character who lived to the ripe old age of ninety-seven. Captain Art hardly made it all when Black diphtheria in his grandfather's family took the lives of four young children in fifteen days back in the fall of 1889.

When the native Bostonian, Calvin S. Parker, came to Long Lake in March, 1858, he went straight to Bill and Rachel Helms' clearing on Forked Lake. Here, Bill had erected a two-room log cabin with garret, in which he somehow managed to house six young children, a servant girl, two regular boarders, and four hounds. Parker became a permanent guest of the hunter and trapper and his wife.

Captain Parker was a mild and gentle person, six feet, two inches tall, with long, unkempt beard that waved in the wind, and equally long hair which he parted in the middle. He carried a single-barreled gun almost as long as himself and wore a long hunting knife rudely fashioned from a broken sword. A graduate of Williams College, he claimed to have studied medicine for two and a half years at Pittsfield, Mass. Although dignified in Long Lake's 1892 census as "M.D.," he is never known to have practised his profession. Instead, he was ever "a-huntin' and a-trappin'," as he himself said. He and Bill Helms trapped in winter, hunted in summer and fall, and fished in spring.

Captain Parker had once been employed by the Hudson Bay Company and long carried one of its guns. He had crossed the western prairies, an attaché at one time of Kit Carson's band. In an Indian attack, he once saw Kit shoot two Indians and carve up three more. A glow would come to his face when he spoke of Carson.

"Gad, he is a customer," he would say, as he slapped his tattered leggings, "and you may guess he hates them varmints, the Crows and Blackfeet Indians."

An accomplished musician, the captain would often play the saxophone to the lively accompaniment of Bill Helms' clarinet. The unearthly stillness of Forked Lake was shattered with their loud, echoing music each night.

Captain Parker was never a hermit in the usual sense.

Though he renounced urban living for the quiet of the mountains, he sought companionship constantly and was always in contact with his wife. A school-teacher in Boston, Permelia Parker visited her husband's mountain haunts at irregular intervals. Later, she succumbed to his chosen mode of living at Long Lake. The two seldom maintained a permanent home.

By 1870, the Calvin Parkers had moved to Newcomb, where the captain was employed at John David's "Halfway House." Parker guided city sportsmen and led his own quadrille band at occasional dances. Often-times, he took his cornet while guiding parties in the woods and enlivened periods of poor weather with impromptu music.

The story was told by A. F. Tait, the noted Adirondack artist of Long Lake, that Captain Parker took the wrong fork of the stream while guiding him into the inlet of Shallow Lake. After struggling for hours in the depthless channel, they reached a dismal swamp and were forced to return. Back at the stream's junction, Captain Parker placed a guide post with rudely inscribed sign, "Take this stream for Shallow Lake." Intentionally or not, the sign pointed in the wrong direction. Immediately, a party of men followed the sign's advice and were forced to spend the night in the swamp.

The old captain's story of awakening from a nap one day to see a ferocious panther swimming dangerously over his head was long remembered. Instantly alert, the guide fired two useless shots into the air. The panther turned out to be a huge black punkie comfortably ensconced in his eyebrows and enjoying tasty nourishment from his upper lid.

In 1876, Captain Parker assumed management of old "Aunt Polly's Inn" at Newcomb. By 1880, they were living with Ike Kenwell at his two-story log building variously called the "Raquette Lake House" or Kenwell Hotel on Raquette Lake.

Parker remained for the duration of his life in the Town of Long Lake, to be described as character and wag. He died January 24, 1912 and is buried in the cemetery there.

The new Captain Parker promises not to live up to the unusual reputation of his older counterpart, but his own and his son's knowledge of woodsmanship takes no back seat. When ninety-six-year-old Willard Sutton injured himself in a fall at remote Brandreth Lake last winter, Captain Art despatched his son, Doug, with Stephen Jennings and George Boudreau in a jeep. The three Emergency and Rescue Squad members drove the hazardous twenty-seven miles from Long Lake to Brandreth, six miles over log roads, in twenty inches of snow. Sutton was in a state of shock, when reached, and pain and uncertain injuries made use of a stretcher impossible. Seated in his favorite platform rocker, the ailing, aged man was brought out of the woods and ultimately to the hospital at Tupper Lake. There the old man died, but not before he had been assured all possible treatment for his wounds.

Somehow it all represents the complete rounding of the circle. Captain Parker of Long Lake carries on.

THE ONLY HANGING IN HAMILTON COUNTY

THERE PROBABLY wasn't a family in all of Hamilton County with a more tempestuous life than that of Edward and Mary Earl. A native of Virginia who had settled at Hope Falls, Ed married Rand Burgess' daughter in October, 1868. Soon after, he returned to heavy drinking, although he frequently made heroic attempts to reform. Meantime, Mary was unfaithful to him for the embrace of the illiterate Bill Hall.

A daughter and a son were born to Edward and Mary Earl. Finally, another daughter, June, named for the month of her birth, was born in 1875. The two oldest children died and were buried in the little graveyard by the old schoolhouse at Hope Falls. Despite Mary Earl's infidelity and Ed's drunken sprees, the two remained together as husband and wife for the sake of their youngest daughter, whom Earl adored.

Ed Earl worked as blacksmith in the Hope Falls firm of Smith & Ressigue, tanners and lumbermen. When the work was dull, he would keep shanty for a lumberman named George Brown up near the Warren County line. Mary Earl succumbed to the charms of her husband's employer.

The violent quarrel that ensued when Ed learned of his wife's most recent infidelity ended before the grand jury of Fulton County. Mary accused her husband of assault with a knife.

Earl consistently protested his innocence. Later, his wife signed a statement that her testimony before the grand jury to procure his indictment was false. Nevertheless, an embittered Edward Earl was sent to Dannemora Prison for three and a half years.

Then and there, Edward Earl made a vow. "When that woman took the witness stand in the courtroom at Johnstown and swore to that she knew was false, she did it coolly and deliberately, and at the instigation of George Brown," he later wrote. "As I looked her in the face, I swore then and there that I would take her life at the cost of my own . . . As her eyes rested on mine, she felt assured that her death at my hands was merely a question as to my getting out of prison alive."

The prison experience did little to dull the determination of the sensitive, moody man. Edward Earl was released from Dannemora on November 19, 1880. He visited briefly the place where he had worked at Hope Falls, but all seemed changed. He found no comfort there.

Meantime, Mary Earl had gone to live with the one-legged George Brown. To them, a daughter was born.

One cold winter's day, Ed Earl walked fourteen miles through the snow to the barn behind Brown's house and stood watching his beloved little daughter, June, come out to slide on her handsleigh. Then he went away. But his brooding continued.

On February 14, 1881, he went to Brown's house and begged his wife to let him have their child. Mary refused.

Three days later, he stole a beam knife from the tannery. It was fourteen inches long, in the shape of a butcher knife, and was used for shaving the hair from the skins that were to be tanned.

On the night of Wednesday, February 16th, he entered the Brown barn. "Next day, the woman came to the barn several times," he later wrote. "Twice she was so near me I could touch her with my hand; once she carried away part of the straw on which I lay concealed."

Cold and hungry, Earl left by the back door, leaving the door unhooked, and spent the night at Rand Burgess' house.

The next morning, he returned. This time, Mary Earl approached the barn apprehensively. She had discovered the unlatched door. There was no time for him to hide. Ed Earl retreated to a vacant stall that opened on the barn floor. Mary Earl gathered some hay and threw it to the cow. Then, taking a pitchfork, she began to feed the horses.

"While she was feeding hay to the colt that stood in the stall next to me, our gaze met," Earl told. "I rushed out and placed myself between her and the small door. As I did so, she struck a wild, impulsive blow with the fork. Poor woman, she thought her last hour had come. She knelt on the floor and begged piteously that I would spare her life . . .

"She told me that she would not mention that I had been in the barn. She would go, get the child and follow me—only spare her life. I stared in her face and knew better.

" 'For God's sake, for the sake of our little dead children, have mercy on me.' "

The plea brought up her husband with a start. Throwing the knife at her feet, he stalked out the door. For a moment, he stood there undecided. Thinking he had left, Mary rose to her feet and rushed madly from the door crying: "George! George!" Ed Earl was galvanized by the shrill sound of the hated name.

"I was no longer human," he wrote. "I was a demon, knowing nothing, fearing nothing, wild!

"I rushed through the barn. She tripped in the door, fell. I snatched the knife from her hand, and did I strike? No. It was the years of suffering, woe, shame, dishonor, the desolate home, injustice, and the hated name of George that held the knife and impelled the blow, as she shrieked, 'Murderer!' "

The knife was driven nearly through the body of Mary Earl, severing every artery around the heart.

For a moment, the enraged man stood in stupefied horror; then he started to run, the cry of murder ringing in his ears. Stumbling across the snow-covered fields, he realized that he still carried the blood-drenched weapon. Hastily, he hurled it from him. He was conscious of passing the graveyard where his two little children lay buried. Looking back, he seemed to see once more the slow, timid step, the pitifully pleading look of his murdered wife. Slowly, he sank into the snow.

Earl went to Northville and surrendered. He was taken on February 20, 1881 to the Hamilton County jail at Lake Pleasant, where he was indicted for the murder of his wife at the June court of trial in August.

The Hon. R. P. Anibal and former District Attorney J. H. Brownell were appointed to defend the prisoner. Their task was not easy. Anibal suggested a plea of insanity. Continuing to smart under what he considered cruel treatment, Earl was determined to contest the charge on the bold grounds of justifiable homicide. He might be freed and that would lead to his own suicide, he thought. He kept insisting he wanted to die. Earl entered a plea of not guilty.

Interest in the case ran high. The verdict of guilty, rendered on August 22, 1881, was not surprising. But the sentence caused amazement. The prisoner, Edward Earl, was "sentenced by the Court to be hanged by the neck until he be found dead on the 14th day of October between the hours of 10 and 2 o'clock." Never before had there been a hanging in Hamilton County.

Hodges

French Louie, the only Adirondack hermit who
was ever able to live in complete self-reliance.

The Brooks Hotel, Speculator, a village landmark for many years.

Captain Parker, a familiar character at Long Lake for fifty-four years.

Mitchell Sabattis, the original Indian settler of Long Lake.

When the verdict was announced, the prisoner turned to the jury. "Thank you, you have done right," he said. When the sentence was imposed, he told the judge, "I am guilty of no murder."

Back in his cell, the accused had ample time for second-thinking. After notifying Anibal that he wanted to make a confession, he wrote the true story and sent it to the press. "I am ready, willing, impatient to meet the death that is in store for me," he said.

During his last days in prison, Earl wrote several letters and articles. He told of enjoying conversation with a five-year-old playing outside his window, and of seeing John C. Holmes' little daughter, who lived, with her family, at the nearby hotel. He wrote a story of his own children for the young girls. To a friend in New York, he wrote humorously of his approaching hanging.

"They are already engaged in building a fence around the place of execution, and from my window I watch the work, talk with the workmen, and have an idea they dread the day more than I," he wrote. "Let me see. I have fifteen days and some hours to live yet (and let me tell you that is longer than some folks have got), and then there is to be some hanging done, i.e., a tight rope performance. I am to be the principal actor in the performance, and am dependent on mostly to make the thing interesting. In fact, I am to act the part of 'the hanged,' and, of course, I shall use my utmost endeavors to act my part in a manner that will give entire satisfaction to all those who are fortunate enough to witness the perform-ance. By the way, were you ever hanged? No? I never was either . . .

"It is a new business to me. I have not the hang of it yet, and I have some misgivings about the results. It may be the death of me; in fact, I have heard instances of persons actually dying while performing in that kind of way. But we are to have a skillful physician in attendance, whose duty it will be to prevent the thing from going too far. The performance will commence about 10 A.M., October 14th, and continue as long as the law directs and physicians think proper . . . Positively, my last appearance in public. No postponement on account of the weather."

The letter was published in a New York newspaper under the headline, "A Jacose Fiend . . . Facetious Under the Shadow of the Gallows."

A crowd of a thousand people gathered at the court house site on Friday, October 14, 1881 to see Earl hanged on the same scaffold that had been used earlier to hang the murderer, Sam Steenburgh of Montgomery County. They were conscious, it seemed, of witnessing history being made. Only a relative few were admitted to the enclosure, fifty-eight feet by forty-eight feet, where the execution took place.

Just after 11 o'clock, Edward Earl marched manfully to the scaffold. The rope was adjusted around his neck and his legs and arms were pinioned. He turned and thanked all the officers for their kindness to him. He bore no ill will toward anyone; he wanted to die, he said. Death would release him from his troubles.

Just before the black cap was drawn over his face, he spoke again.

"I have one thing more to say. If any of you boys ever meet my little girl, please give her at least one kind word. It may do her good and won't cost you anything."

Then, turning to Sheriff Patrick Mitchell, he added, "Sheriff, I am ready. Good-bye, all."

It is told that sobs were heard all around when Earl made his last touching plea to "the boys," and tears fell from the eyes of strong, hardy men who were seldom moved or affected. No doubt those great brawny and bronzed lumbermen spoke many kind words to little June thereafter.

The trap of the gallows was sprung and the weight fell at 11:35. Death ensued at 11:44 and the body was laid in its coffin at 11:47. Edward Earl's body, as he had foretold, was on its way to Hope Falls to stay. Edward Earl's restless spirit was free.

Rand Burgess refused to allow Earl's body to be placed beside his daughter's within the wire enclosure that encircled her grave. Instead, the husband's remains were placed toward the back of the cemetery lot. Now the wire enclosure is gone. Two long low lumps of earth in the shape of a disjointed "T" beside the stone wall of the Hope Falls Cemetery tell mutely where the cruelly murdered Mary Earl and her sorely tormented husband are at rest.

THE BIGGEST LOAD OF LOGS

MANY YEARS AGO, in early spring, when the sun began to warm the land and the once sturdy ice became porous in the lakes, people watched for the annual event.

The waterways were filled with moving logs. Down the inlet from Sacandaga Lake they came. The waters of Lake Pleasant were hidden under a mass of brown bark and skinned hemlock, as the fruit of a winter's work floated majestically toward the narrow inlet. Down the Kunjamuck River came the logs and into the Sacandaga headwaters. From here, they were driven down the full length of the roaring Sacandaga to the Hudson River and the insatiable lumber mills at Glens Falls.

The endless need for lumber to serve a growing nation was not easily satisfied. The small local mills of an earlier day were inadequate to supply the unquenchable demand. The tremendous forest reserves of the Adirondacks stood ready. The rivers were at hand for convenient transportation.

Log riders stood precariously on the floating logs and poled their way along the shore to free logs that became caught. The less-skilled rode a "cooter," two logs bound together with rope or pliable birch saplings.

"The first spring I ever drove lumber, I was in the water most of the time," says Shelah Page of Speculator, now in his 85th year. "But I decided to learn to ride the logs and was encouraged to keep it up. About the fifth day, I had begun to master it pretty well."

Similarly, George Perkins, who had just arrived from Warren County, hired some men from Newton's Corners and took a contract to drive Carpenter's logs down the Jessup.

"We were in and out of the river all day, and that night we slept on the bank in the snow," George told. "I swam far enough to cover the length of Jessup's River."

Flood dams along the upper reaches of the Sacandaga, at Burnham Mills, at Robb's Creek, and at the junction of the East Branch with the main channel, continued the movement of the logs to market. There was a big river-driving camp above the falls at Augur Flats. From sixty to seventy men worked the river to get the logs through.

A flood dam at Girard's in Griffin served George Hutchins, George Springs, Clarence Brooks and others who lumbered up the East Branch. The Indian Lake lumbermen used to mark and measure every log before sending it down-river. You never could be sure about the mill folks down Northville way.

The high flood dams were equipped with sluices closed by a plank and with a platform at the top. At the appropriate moment, one man would loosen the plank with a peavey hook, while a second hauled on a rope to lift the board high. George Wager of Wells tended the lower dam. Russell Berry was once at Burnham Mills with a young helper who wanted to have his new woolen shirt cleaned. Berry advised him to tie a string to the collar and leave the shirt in the flume while he tripped the dam. When the flood waters finally subsided, the unhappy youth found nothing but the collar of his shirt on the end of the string.

Most of the older mountain men engaged in lumbering at one time or another in their lifetimes.

Fifty or sixty years ago, there was nothing to do but work in the lumber woods, says Selah Page. "I went into the woods at the age of fourteen. There was nothing to do here. You couldn't even get an education. We had school districts. One school was located on the back road and all we did day after day was make applesauce."

It was rugged work. The lumbering schedule called for road-building in the summer and fall, then for log-skidding until Christmas time. The men would then come out of the woods for a week, only to return for a good three months. "Unless we were called out by sickness, we wouldn't get out again until late March," Selah relates. "We used to like to make it out by mid-March though, because there was usually a St. Patrick's Day dance at one of the local hotels."

Breakfast at George Perkins' camp was served at 3 A.M. and work started at 3:30. The day at Ernie Brooks' camp began an hour earlier. Pay averaged about a dollar a day with board.

During the winter, the roads were kept open by a lightly loaded sled to make tracks through the snow. A sprinkler wagon was used when the roads became too deeply rutted. It was a sled containing a tank of water with two taps with wooden plugs. When the plugs were pulled, the water filled the ruts and froze solid. One tank would cover from a quarter to three-quarters of a mile.

It was Ashley Perkins' job to fill the barrels one season at his father's camp. "It would be thirty below zero and the water would be running down my arms," Ashley tells.

Ingenuity often produced small comforts. Bill Simons of Wells, working as a road monk, once acquired a deer killed out of season. The meat was secretly "jerked" over a slow, smokeless fire in a nearby thicket.

"If you see me climb on the snowbank, that's the signal,"

Bill would say. At such times, a hot piece of venison would be placed in Ashley's hand.

Appetites were voracious. "We would get out of bed and wolf down meat and beans, go out and work, come in for a mammoth noonday meal, go back and work, and come right back for another hearty meal," declares Selah Page.

"There would be twenty-five teams and seventy-five men. They were lousier than pet coons. There's a way to avoid lice, though. Take camphor gum and hang it around your neck and maybe carry a piece in your pocket and they won't bother you."

Selah Page is credited with having cut the biggest log and having dragged the biggest load of logs in Hamilton County.

In 1914, he was drawing logs near Sacandaga Lake. That was the spring that a record load of 157 logs was hauled five miles by the men of another nearby lumber camp and unloaded on the lake. Verne Pelcher's bob was used, and the team of Nathaniel Ingram of Hope Falls, who was the driver.

Hailed as at least one of the biggest loads of logs ever drawn in the Southern Adirondack lumber region, the event was given full publicity.

"Mr. Ingram, who is only 22 years of age, is considered an expert reinsman and one of the best log drawers in the county," the newspaper accounts read. "The estimated number of feet in the load was 35 markets (a market designated a log sixteen inches in diameter at the small end and thirteen feet long). The logs were loaded from the skidway onto sleighs with eight-foot bunks and were just thirteen feet high from the top of the bunk."

The men in Selah Page's camp were completely galled at such crass competition. Certain that they could outdo any such record, they urged Selah to take up the challenge. Selah refused.

"But the next year, they kept asking me to try, and by this time I was ready," Selah relates.

George Perkins, as boss, was less enthusiastic. It would be

much too expensive if the logs were dropped and had to be reloaded, he pointed out. But when the men assured him that, in such case, they would all work on Sunday on their own time to pick up the timber, if it spilled. George had no reasons to object to the try.

The men got thirteen toggle chains and worked furiously all day. At length, they had loaded 220 logs. Now it was Selah's turn. Slowly and ponderously, the tremendous weight was pulled across the rough, snowy ground, to be landed safely on the Sacandaga Lake banking ground.

It was a big event and a triumph for the lumbering group. The record has never been exceeded.

Selah's biggest log was a five market, and he cut it up the Kunjamuck in Oregon.

Lumbering made for lusty men. Working at Mud Lake in 1914, Ashley Perkins rose at 3 A.M. and shovelled snow all day. "At quitting time, I went out to the Indian Lake road, walked to Wells to a dance over the old *Adirondack Record* office at Wells, walked two miles home with a girl, and got back in time for work. It was all of sixteen miles one way and I wasn't tired at all."

Laboring as young men in the lumber woods at Indian Lake, Selah Page, together with Erne Culver and Bill Bradt of Wells and Pat McDonald of Indian Lake, used to walk down to Speculator each week to the dance platform in the grove near Martin Kelly's hotel. "We'd come walking out nine miles, dance until 2 A.M., and walk back in time for breakfast, and go to work," Selah states.

George Perkins used to leave the lumber woods to take his family to Pottersville and the Warren County Fair. There they would see a fellow named Cunningham, a good runner, who used to follow the fairs, entering the foot-races, and taking the prize money. One year, George could stand it no longer. Peeling off his shoes, he ran the race in his stocking feet, ably defeating Cunningham and copping the three-hundred-dollar prize.

There was boon companionship, too. After working in a lumber camp at Jessup's River, Arthur Perry and "Pants" Lawrence came to the Speculator House on their way to visit the city the following day. Here they met two lumberjacks who had spent their money and were on their return trip to camp.

A poker game was organized, Pants and Art lending their opponents five dollars each.

"They cleaned us right out," Pants told. "Art and I started back for camp and they went to Amsterdam."

"Art, you dead-broke?" Pants asked, as they approached camp.

"I haven't got a nickel," was Art's sad reply.

"Art, I've got a quarter and a dime, but we're going to start even," Pants told his comrade, and straightway he threw his coins over the top of the barn.

The Adirondack men themselves were the mainstays of the lumbering operations. But additional workers were required. Many came from Canada. Others were recruited from the city taverns with promises of adventure and good monetary return. No one knew much about the background of many of the new-comers. And when, as sometimes happened, they were killed by accident or occasional suicide, the official records were brief and without relatives being named.

When proximity to settlements permitted the men to leave the woods on Saturday nights, they were ready for bear. During the period of lumbering operations at Piseco, there were over a dozen saloons located within a distance of eight miles. They were always filled with men thirsty for drink and ready for an animated conversation that often-times climaxed in bloody battle. The old Speculator House was described as a battleground for lumbermen in the days when it was run by Pants Lawrence—the easiest place in the world to get an argument underway. Yet strict courtesy to women was well-observed.

The tradition continued.

"Mayor William Remney announces that Speculator has started a drive against drunken lawlessness in this village with the arrest and conviction of four lumberjacks who will spend the next thirty days in the county jail," read an article in the *Hamilton County Record* of July 5, 1945. "It becomes a habit with some of the lumberjacks to come to this village periodically, become intoxicated at the local bar and then proceed to make public nuisances of themselves for a time, a practice which Mayor Remney declares must stop at once or the offenders will join the four in jail."

At night, as they lounged around the bunkhouse at camp, the different men would be called on to sing a song. This was particularly the case on Saturday nights, since the lumbermen could sleep a little longer the next day. One of the favorites was "Garrison Rock" and the men listened with satisfaction to the well-remembered words:

> " 'Twas on one Monday's morning
> In the springtime of the year . . ."

More earthly was the song composed in dubious honor of the lumber camp cook:

> "She came rolling home in the morning
> With shoes and stockings in her hand,
> She'd been out all night
> 'Til broad daylight
> With the Sacandaga gang—"

It took courage and strength to endure the rigors of the work. No doctors were at hand. Accident insurance and workmen's compensation were unheard of. "If you cut yourself with an axe, you healed yourself," says Selah. "I have scars on my feet and lower and upper leg."

Fatal accidents were fairly frequent. "Whocky" Arnold of Hope Falls tells that his grandfather, Aaron "Bub" Arnold, was killed in 1884 by logs rolling down a bank. Five years later, Fabius Arnold, Wocky's uncle, was killed at the age of twenty-six when struck by a falling tree at Piseco. Lewis Burgess, a neighbor, died when struck by a binder on the logs. Oddest of all, Seymour Brownell's brother was killed in a lumbering accident and when Seymour came out of the woods to tell his mother, he found her dead. Tragedy occurred in January, 1946, just after Robb and Nina Morrison's son, Richard, had safely returned after twenty months' combat service in Europe. While unloading a truck at the Carl Miller Lumber Yard in Speculator, he was instantly killed when a log slipped and crushed his skull.

Lumbering continues in the Adirondacks. But, like other modern industries, the preponderance is now done under the auspices of larger firms such as Finch, Pruyn & Company and the International Paper Company, both of which maintain large holdings in the lower Adirondacks.

AN ADIRONDACK LUMBERMAN

INTO THE SMALL HOTEL in a village in St. Lawrence County walked a short, unprepossessing-looking man. Lifting unshaven face to the desk clerk, he asked for a room for the night.

Quickly, the clerk surveyed the undesirable—unbuckled overshoes, unkempt woodsmen's clothing, and the characteristic chew of tobacco that wadded his cheek. The hotelman was sorry; there wasn't a room in the house.

Wordlessly, the small man rocked back on his heels while reaching into his pocket and drawing out a roll of bills that obviously totalled into the thousands. Thoughtfully, he thumbed the hundred-dollar notes.

The desk clerk suddenly remembered any one of several accommodations that might be at this honored guest's disposal. The newly-arrived was hurriedly shown to his room.

The experience was typical. The man was Lumberman

Ernie Brooks from Newton's Corners, on a horse-buying mission to the northern part of the State.

Ernie, who was born at Indian Lake of Joel and Helen Morehouse Brooks, was a woodsman from the start. In a period when local lumbering was in its heyday in the Adirondacks, Ernie helped to give it dignity and color. He and his brothers, Ed and Clarence, lumbered for years at Indian Lake, Ernie and Ed joining forces to form the Brooks Brothers Lumber Company there. Not content with lumbering alone, Ernie was a hotelman on the side.

Up at Indian Lake, Ernie was married to Myra O'Kane. When she died after bearing him four children, he moved his family down to Newton's Corners in the Town of Lake Pleasant and later married Nathan and Mary Satterlee Page's daughter, Nora. Together, they ran the old Brooks Hotel south of the four corners and raised a family of five.

Ernie's reputation as a lumberman was a good one. None worked his men harder. None offered better pay. A man knew, when he signed with Brooks, that he was to maintain an active life throughout the long winter months in the mountains.

There was a reason. One winter, over on Sacandaga Lake, Ernie misjudged the weather and, before he could get his logs banked, the spring thaw set in. The logs lay on the ground throughout the following summer and the family lacked the income that was so badly needed. It was a bitter lesson that Ernie never forgot. After that, he worked himself and his men with fury to be sure always to make the drive on time.

Selah Page worked for Ernie in the winter of 1916 at Coon Creek near the third bridge on the road to Wells.

"We used to pull the horses out at 2 A.M. and wouldn't see camp until dark. I'll give Ernie credit, though. He was out with the head team and came back with the hind team each day. And he paid good money. But the work was just too hard. I said, if I can't make a living easier than that, I'm going to starve. After that, I did freighting for the camps but never lumbered again."

One evening, a call came for Dr. Joseph Head to go to the Brooks camp to treat a sick lumberjack. By the time he had bounced over the rough woods' roads to reach his destination, it was the middle of the night. To his amazement, the men were already at breakfast. Ernie himself had appeared at midnight for his morning chow.

Dr. Head sat relaxing over a cup of strong hot coffee. Nearby sat Jerry Murphy, a rugged lumberjack known for the quality of his work.

"Yes sir, I'm going to quit," Murphy told the physician. "Ernie promised me a full-time job and we're sleeping a couple of hours every night. That's no full-time job. I'm through."

Each day, the clocks at camp were set a few minutes further ahead, so the men would not complain too bitterly about their early rising hour. One winter night, the men had just completed drawing logs and were wolfing down their evening meal. It was 9 o'clock in the evening but the clock read 12.

Allie O'Kane of Indian Lake sat eating with his boss.

"Ernie," he drawled, "if you don't change that clock pretty soon, it's going to be Fourth of July before the snow goes off."

Ernie could laugh with the others, but his firm discipline never faltered.

Once, while lumbering at Cannon Brook, the lumberman came out of the woods and procured a rooster. It would start crowing daily at 4 A.M. Ernie called it his alarm clock. Thoroughly annoyed after several days' repetition of this newly-found reveille, the boys decided that something must be done. The next day, the lifeless rooster hung on the knob of the bunkhouse door. Ernie was silent, but soon returned with a second rooster.

"The one who kills that bird is fired," he announced.

The rooster remained alive.

Allie O'Kane and Henry Brooks were once working at a skidway. They had successfully placed about 3,000 pieces of heavy timber on the skidway when a big tree twisted and became wedged. It was mighty irksome. Allie grumbled that he'd be darned if he would move the offensive tree. He wasn't being paid for such work, he declared, and the two continued piling logs.

Two days later, the observant Ernie confronted his two employees.

"A couple of the men are sick," he told them, no doubt smiling to himself. "I'll have to ask you to unload."

Embittered but helpless, Allie and Henry worked themselves to a frenzy moving each log by hand, because the wedged tree had not earlier been removed.

The lumberjacks were loyal to Ernie. One thing they knew, as they performed the back-breaking labor hours on end: They would always be paid generously. You could always depend on Ernie to pull the job through. His innate fairness and human understanding made him further championed among his men.

"Ernie once left me back in the woods to cut lumber for him," Sandford Courtney has told. "He left me twenty-five dollars worth of food. When he came to settle, he paid me for more work than I'd done and more than the marker estimated. That's the way Ernie was."

The lumberman had a way with people that could not be denied.

Hi Craig of Wells, an accomplished wood-cutter, had always worked at lumbering but he had decided to work at something else, at least for a time. Hi was working in a glove shop at Wells, when Brooks arrived to ask the woodsman and his wife to take charge at his lumber camp headquarters.

"I'm not going to work in a lumber camp," Hi told him with determination. At the same time, he realized the need for money to build a house. Ernie's guarantee of $1,000 sounded good.

"I'll give you a week to make up your mind," Ernie said.

Wavering somewhat, Hi agreed to leave the decision to his wife. Ernie knew he had won his case.

The Craigs took the job, but only on the agreement that Hi could have his old job of cutting wood.

One day, Ernie came to him, characteristically chewing tobacco.

"You'll have to come to camp," he instructed the wood-cutter. "I just fired a choreboy."

Hi fumed. "I told you I wouldn't be choreboy," he protested.

Ernie set to work on Hi's better instincts. The choreboy had been lazy, making the work too hard for Mrs. Craig, he explained.

Reluctantly, Hi left his axe to go back to camp.

"At the end of the season, Ernie gave us a bonus and told us to stay and rest for a couple of days," Hi tells. When the two protested, Ernie insisted that they had saved him a great deal of money by getting the men up and out on time.

Brooks' sense of humor was well-recognized.

Back at Newton's Corners, now known by the new-fangled name of Speculator, he liked to leave his hotel of an evening to stop in at Robb Stuart's general store. It was the typical country gathering place, where the men sat on a winter's night, telling stories while they chewed tobacco and spat at the stove.

One night, the lumberman and a companion hit upon a well-laid plan. First one, then the other, would cough and sneeze, commenting on the bad colds they had acquired. Listening with apprehension, Robb finally concluded that he, too, was coming down with a severe cold. Robb sneezed a couple of times, went straight to bed and called the doctor.

One day, Ernie was walking down the road with a bag in his hand. Amelia Wilber wanted to know what the bag contained.

"Beechnuts," replied the lumberman promptly. What's more, they weren't old beechnuts, he told her, but just freshly picked that winter's day. He explained that the beechnuts had stayed on some of the trees and, when the wind blew, they were coming down and rolling into the hollow in the snow at the base of the trees.

A short time later, Ernie chuckled inwardly as he watched Amelia and some youngsters walking up the road. Amelia carried an empty bag in her hand.

A legend ended in 1935. Forest fires raged along the mountains surrounding the Sacandaga Reservoir and all forest rangers were called to assist. It was at the time that the mother of Halsey Page, the local forest ranger, died. Halsey asked Ernie to go in his place while he attended the funeral.

The fire-fighters were to be taken across the reservoir by boat. When they were ready to set out, it was obvious to Ernie that the craft was badly overloaded. Out on the water, the boat rocked precariously with each movement of its occupants. Suddenly, it overturned, dumping its human cargo into the deep waters of the lake. Five men were drowned.

Ernie Brooks had died in his sixty-third year. Neighbors at Speculator felt that somehow an age had ended.

FIRST ON DECK

EVERYONE liked to see Allie O'Kane of Indian Lake join a group of conversers. Known for his unusual experiences, it was interesting to guess what the Central Adirondack lumberjack would tell his companions next.

Allie was lumbering up near Colvin Mountain one winter. The weather turned mighty frigid; so cold, in fact, that Allie couldn't even light his pipe from the blow-torch the company provided.

He was out fishing on Little Moose Pond near Indian Clearing when a thunderstorm suddenly struck. The weather turned bitterly cold and the lake's surface quickly froze. Allie pulled his boat across the lake's solid surface, gathering up frozen fish.

Then, to his surprise, he came right up against three licks of lightning frozen entirely static right there in the ice.

One day, Ernie Brooks, Allie and a group were going to Rock Pond up Oregon way for some fishing. Before they had hit the trail, some time had been spent at the Speculator hotel run by Jack Buyce. Underway at last, they had only reached nearby Elm Lake when darkness fell. As happy as were many of their number, it seemed the better part of wisdom to bed down for the night.

Allie O'Kane passed out. His companions decided it would be good fun to move his inert body to the aged brick vault that Phillip Rhinelander had built so long ago to contain the body of his deceased wife.

Allie came to life the following morning, his eyes staring blearily toward the peeling paint of the celestial scene on the ceiling. Beneath was the title, "Resurrection Morning."

Allie did a double take. "Holy Mackinaw," he was heard to murmur, "it's resurrection morning and I'm the first man on deck."

BRIGHTSIDE-ON-RAQUETTE

THE CENTRAL ADIRONDACKS were beginning to prosper under the magic touch of William West Durant when in 1882 Joseph O. A. Bryere arrived from Three Rivers, Canada, by way of Waterbury, Conn., to settle at Raquette Lake. Joe was twenty-two years old and ambitious to make the most of the opportunities afforded by the increasing numbers of summer people arriving in the area. Durant was encouraging the beginnings of new and larger hostelries to accommodate the seasonal influx.

William Durant's brother, Charles, had recently acquired Osprey Island from the hermit-huntsman, Alvah Dunning, and

Barn Where Mary Earl was Murdered at Hope Falls on February 17, 1881.

Willard Letson's Cabin on Gilman Lake across from the ill-fated Klondike House.

Brightside-on-Raquette, built by Joe Bryere and his bride with logs cut by their own hands.

Holland House, Blue Mountain Lake, one of the noted hotels in the golden era.

was building "Fairview" Camp. Joe Bryere became its care-taker.

Raquette Lake was a wilderness setting in those days. A young fellow had to go over to Blue Mountain Lake to mingle with people and to find fun. One summer day, when Joe was over at Blue Mountain, he was introduced to Mary Agnes Gooley, a young Albany resident of twenty-one who was employed at the magnificent Prospect House. Joe was pleased when Agnes decided to spend the following winter with the family of George W. Turnicliff, proprietor of the hotel. Joe visited her often. And in the spring, when Agnes left briefly for Albany, he knew she was the one person from whom he could never be parted for long.

Joseph O. A. Bryere and Mary Agnes Gooley became the first couple to be married at Raquette Lake. A priest from Troy performed the ceremony at Ed Bennett's inn, "Under the Hemlocks," on July 8, 1884. The marriage certificate was written on the official stationery of the hotel.

Agnes Bryere's wedding corsage was a pond lily. Her honeymoon trip was a boat ride on Raquette Lake. The newlyweds made their way to Charlie Durant's boathouse, which was to be their first home.

Marriage was not the only factor in Joe Bryere's plans. The increasing numbers of city visitors to the area caused him to persist in his idea to become an Adirondack boarding-house proprietor by the fastest available means. He had already selected a site on Indian Point, which could be simply obtained by exercising squatter's rights.

Joe saved the ends of logs left over from the construction of Charlie Durant's place and got them moved to his chosen location. In 1884, Joe and Agnes began to clear their land of trees, snaking the trunks to the lake and making them into a boom, which they towed by guideboat to the sawmill at the foot of the lake. The logs were cut into lumber and delivered back by steamboat.

Soon, Joe's inn began to emerge in the form of a little, open camp. A small two-room cottage was added, and finally a house for the family. Brightside-on-Raquette had begun. Joe's dream was realized when the doors were opened to the public on May 14, 1891.

Local people were the principal visitors for the first two months. Robert Dunning, the carpenter, and his wife, Octavia, came with C. H. Hendy and Henry Callahan from Forked Lake. From Blue Mountain Lake came Melvin Burnham, Henry Taylor, John McLaughlin, Duane Fuller, Joe Cross and Pat Heiney. The still-existent guest book shows Chauncey Hathorn, Amos and Charlie Blanchard, Frank Wood, Seth Pierce, and D. La Prairie as early visitors from Raquette. And the guides, Calvin Town, Willard Sutton, Ed Martin, B. F. Emerson and Riley Plumley came over from Long Lake way. The paying guests began to arrive.

Business was making rapid strides at Raquette Lake by 1894. Brightside-on-Raquette was one of five inns on the lake, taking its place beside Charlie Bennett's pretentious "The Antlers" and famous "Hemlocks," Joseph Whitney's "Honest Joe's" and Charlie Blanchard's "Wigwams." The Bryere establishment afforded cozy accommodations for thirty guests, who paid seventy-five cents for meals or from twelve to eighteen dollars weekly for room and board. Its tennis courts offered further inducement.

"Brightside-on-Raquette displays its trim and artistic proportions on the south side of Indian Point, beneath the shadows of numerous trees," said *Wallace's Adirondack Guide* of 1894. "Within and without, in finish and decoration, it is a piece of rustic beauty, and indicates that the owner and builder possesses rare skill in the art of building and equipment."

A serious set-back came for the Joseph Bryeres early in the present century when Brightside was destroyed by fire at the height of the Adirondacks' golden age. Joe had it quickly rebuilt to accommodate guests and the business continued.

The place made for interesting, wholesome living for the four Bryere children, born between 1887 and 1894. The original village of Raquette Lake had started over on Long Point with Durant's new post office, a church, a store run by John McLaughlin, and the telegraph office operated by Morris Callahan. The place was reached by an old wood road in winter and, in other seasons, by boat.

A school was started on the original J. Pierpont Morgan property with Arthur Martin, brother of the guide, as first teacher. Local children were recruited to swell the ranks of scholars to that size necessary for official recognition. Mrs. Dennis Dillon recalls their being required to sit and hold a book to impress the visiting inspectors.

For the first five years, the students were brought to the school by boat. The teachers lived at Brightside, using a guide boat for their own and the Bryere children's transportation. In 1897, Judge Dillon became the teacher.

For the Bryere youngsters, there were colorful visitors to Brightside at all seasons of the year. "Uncle" Seth Pierce, the neat old hermit with the little white beard who lived in a closed-in lean-to on the rear of the J. Harvey Ladew property, always came for Christmas, Clara Bryere recalls. "On Christmas morning, each of us children would stand on a step of the enclosed stairway of the inn, Uncle Seth, dressed in his Civil War uniform, at the top. It was a regular rite with us."

Pete Tromblee, the Indian, was at hand and delighted the children with his overheard reply to the inquiring "who-who" of an owl, "This is me, Pete Tromblee; who in hell are you?" A peddler drove his shabby horse and rickety sleigh across the ice in winter to demonstrate glistening pots and pans never before seen by the children except in kitchen use. Each spring, Nell McGinn of Indian Lake would row from house to house in a guide boat to sell, from her big Saratoga trunk, the women's hats she had made during the long winter months. And Alonzo Mix, the photographer, would come at intervals to photograph the interior of the inn or the residents themselves. It was happy, carefree living at best.

All this has changed. Joe Bryere died August 1, 1941. Like

its sister hostelries, Brightside is no longer operated commercially. Nor is it yet surrounded by the luxury and magnificence that was Raquette Lake of former years.

The Bryere name remains. Clara Bryere spends her winters in Florida, but yields to the lure of the mountain lake country each spring. Regularly, she travels to market in her shiny new motor boat or to receive personal visitors at the Brightside dock across the bay. For Clara, there is no better place to be. Many former guests of Brightside would agree.

DEATH AT THE KLONDIKE HOUSE

SCARCELY RECOGNIZED among the hotels and boarding houses in and about the Wells-Lake Pleasant area at the turn of the century was a ramshackle structure on the old Gilman road near the head of Mud Lake (now Gilman Lake). Henry Hartman, a burly two-hundred pounder of thirty-seven, was its proprietor.

Hartman had arrived in the community two years earlier from Fulton County's Town of Bleecker to manage the dubious Klondike House. With him had come his "woman." Formal records named her Birdsell J. Hartman, twenty-nine, land-lady of the hotel. Local folks knew her as "Bird" Redmond, who had taken up living with Hartman without benefit of matrimony.

Bird had formerly resided in Gloversville, having been employed at a number of places, including the disreputable Hotel Fulton across from the F. J. & G. Railroad station. The place had been destroyed by fire about the time she had left.

Under their joint proprietorship, the Klondike Hotel had borne a consistently unsavoury name.

Nearby on Mud Lake lived sixty-one-year-old Willard Letson, regarded as a hermit, who sometimes served as trusted guide for hunting expeditions and was often employed to do chores for Hartman. A quiet, unassuming man of slight build, he had early acquired the courage of one who has long lived close to nature. Letson was a person who went his own self-reliant way, oblivious to the affairs of others. He was described as a harmless individual, well-liked in the community.

The three formed an unlikely trio, made more so by Hartman's intense jealousy of Letson, whom he often accused of being too intimate with Bird.

The date was Tuesday, May 21, 1906. Hartman had been drawn to serve as trial juror at Hamilton County Court. Reluctantly leaving his hotel in charge of Bird Redmond and Willard Letson, he had come morosely to Lake Pleasant. During the day, he had sat drinking in the local bar until by evening, he had reached a drunken and ugly state.

Letson and Redmond, not to be outdone, had meanwhile enjoyed a drinking bout of their own in the Klondike bar.

Things got mighty rowdy around the Klondike House that night after Hartman's return. Tempers flared and voices were raised in accusations and recriminations. Before it was over, a drunken brawl had ensued. Hartman began to misuse Bird and Letson tried to defend her. Over Letson's protestations, Bird was ejected from the house and went to stay with neighbors. Hartman's rage and jealousy were unbounded.

The deep solitude of the brooding mountains spread ominous quiet over the Klondike House at a late hour that night.

Hartman attended court the following morning, but it was plainly seen that he was intoxicated. He sat limply around the courthouse even after the jurors were dismissed. Then he repaired to the bar of the nearby hotel.

Toward evening, he left the hotel at the head of the lake and proceeded to the Speculator House of Frank "Pants" Lawrence. Here he lounged about the lobby for some time.

"I kind of hate to go home," he said, adding that he was afraid someone might be there to "do" him.

Finally, Dave Arnold, one of the guides who frequented

Lawrence's hotel, offered to accompany him. Hartman was in no shape to go by himself, Dave felt.

The Klondike House was locked when Arnold and Hartman arrived. When entrance was gained, a scene of dishevelment greeted them. The furniture in the common room was overturned and broken, carpets were pulled up, and blood spotted the barroom floor. Blood stains were also found on the stairway and Arnold insisted on searching upstairs.

Trembling visibly, Hartman lighted a kerosene lantern and the two started to mount to the second floor. Hartman's hand was shaking so violently that the glass lamp chimney fell shattering to the floor. Arnold carried the new lamp that was procured and the men moved slowly from room to room.

When the doorway of one particular room was reached, Hartman tried to prevent Arnold from entering. But the young guide was not to be deterred. Throwing open the door, he found the dead body of Letson lying on an old quilt and mangled almost beyond recognition. The head was badly battered and the whole body was bruised and torn.

Hartman expressed surprise and consternation as the two surveyed the results of one of the most brutal of murders.

"Guess we'd better go back to Lake Pleasant and report this to the sheriff," Dave said quietly. Hartman was led dumbly up the road and around the lake to the office of Sheriff Ed Call.

The sheriff, together with Dr. C. J. Dodge, District Attorney Wilson and Assistant District Attorney Eugene D. Scribner, conducted the investigation. They found a pair of trousers and a vest covered with blood. The clothing was readily identified as belonging to Hartman. Fingerprints showed that Hartman had used a towel to dry his blood-stained hands.

A coroner's investigation was immediately ordered and Assistant District Attorney Scribner took the case in hand. Bird Redmond was apprehended at the hotel of John Hartman, brother of the accused, at Bull Run about three miles north of Gloversville, to be held as witness. As the probe proceeded, the character of the mountains occasionally shone through to mingle humor where tragedy held uncertain sway.

Under questioning, Dave Arnold stated that the bathroom at the Klondike House was on the left as he had entered the hotel.

"Then the bathroom was on the right when you left," the assistant district attorney affirmed.

"No sir," replied Arnold.

"But you just said that it was on the left when you went in," Scribner protested.

Arnold raised his eyes levelly with those of his questioner.

"I backed out," the undaunted guide declared.

During the September trial at Lake Pleasant, interest was widespread in view of the sheer brutality of the murder. Public sentiment ran high against Hartman from the beginning. The jury deliberated forty-five minutes before returning a verdict of murder in the second degree.

Hartman was sentenced to life imprisonment at Dannemora Prison by Justice E. A. Spencer. Ultimately, he was pardoned and returned to Gloversville, where he soon died.

On Sunday evening, September 16, 1906, fire of unknown origin completely destroyed the Klondike. Lake Pleasant folks figured it was better that way.

THE VILLAGE BLACKSMITH

FEVERISH ACTIVITY among the American troops in Eastern Germany bespoke the beginnings of a new campaign. The Rhine River had been reached. The bridgehead at Remagen had been secured. Now it was time to move thousands upon thousands of men, materiel and equipment to the eastern side and continue the advance to the German heartland. It was spring of 1945.

Every possible craft of any size was commandeered. The protective smoke covering was in operation. The advance was underway.

Ed Brooks of Lake Pleasant was among the American contingent of troops due for early crossing. As his unit approached the historic river's banks, an officer asked which men knew how to row a boat. Nothing could have better suited a son of the Adirondacks. Ed volunteered at once.

As he crawled to the rower's seat and put oars into oarlocks, Ed chanced to look at a small metal plate on the boat's gunwales.

"Made in Speculator by John F. Buyce," he read. It sounded like home. At least, that is the way Ed told it to a grinning John F. Buyce.

Meanwhile, more than 2,000 miles away in the Town of Lake Pleasant, John F. Buyce, probably the most accomplished craftsman the Southern Adirondacks had ever produced, had found it necessary to discontinue his fabrication of custom-made boats for lack of proper materials. Above all else, John F. insisted on quality. When purest excellence proved impossible, workmanship came to a halt west of Speculator's four corners in John's small shop. Perfection of his prized rowboats had involved two generations of Buyces and the seventy-six-year-old craftsman was not about to substitute an inferior product at this late date.

As choice as it had become, the Lake Pleasant rowboat was only one of the fine products of John F. Buyce's accomplished hands. A true son of the mountains, he had won laudable reputation as a blacksmith while the trade was required. But he was more than that. John lived to become one of the finest representatives of the area in which he lived. He had a way of excelling in whatever work he undertook.

The tradition had started with John's father, Fitch Buyce. An excellent carpenter, Fitch built several of the buildings that early took their place as landmarks in the community, and became an excellent maker of wood products as well. Born in 1843, a son of John Buyce of the Town of Gilman, the big, square-shouldered, good-looking Fitch married Deborah Parslow and built for their occupancy a small log house west of Lake Pleasant Village where Fish Mountain Road cuts off to the north. Here, on May 28, 1869, John F. Buyce was born. Three years later, a second son blessed the union. He was named Alvah W. Meanwhile, Fitch had built a second house for his family near the corners just up the road. It is now the kitchen of the "mousetrap" hotel.

In 1874, when John F. was five years old, the family sold its property and went to Lewey Lake to keep shanty for George Griffin, the lumberman, who then numbered the newly arrived French Louie Seymour as one of his employees.

Later, Fitch and Deborah moved to Squaw Brook near Sabael, where Fitch operated a sawmill. It was here that John F. received his early schooling. Six years later, the family returned to Lake Pleasant and John and Alvah attended school there. Then the family went to Gilmantown, where Fitch started a novelty mill, making broom handles and butter tubs and covers for kegs and barrels. He was to remain active in carpentry until his eightieth year.

Fitch also worked for a time as nightwatchman at Burnham's Mills and protested vehemently when Mrs. Burnham left him the same menu of bread and milk for his midnight snack three nights in a row.

"I like it," the angular Fitch told her, "but you get right sick of it after the first thirty or forty days."

In 1882, the Buyces returned to Newton's Corners and Fitch built a small hotel near the four corners. It prepared him to assist the Osbornes at a later date at their first hotel. Asked to run the place for a couple of days while the family attended a funeral at Fish House, Fitch had open house in the bar.

Marinus Lawrence entered the place tentatively. "Fitch, is my credit good?" he wanted to know.

"Rene, your credit is unlimited," Fitch sang out with the warmest of hospitality. "Step right up, everyone, and have a drink. This is the first time I've been able to buy a drink since Osborne has run the hotel."

His grade schooling completed, John F. had worked for a time with his father as carpenter's helper. Now he opened his first shop in a building constructed entirely by himself. Although it was a crude structure, the building served as workshop and living quarters until 1896, when he built a more comfortable home.

John F. Buyce married Martha J. Slack, eldest daughter of George and Lucinda Brown Slack. To them, a son, Luther Milton, was born in 1898. Martha died December 15, 1911 and in 1912, John traded his home with his brother, Alvah, for the building on the northwest corner of the four corners in Speculator. He had built a blacksmith shop next door to this building in 1919. Now for a time, he ran a general store in conjunction with his business.

When he first started his craft as blacksmith, there was no way to have supplies sent to his shop. John used to tell of starting at dawn to walk ten miles down the old dirt road to Wells to buy a bar of steel and a small supply of blacksmith's coal, which he carried to Newton's Corners in a pack-basket. With these materials, he would forge horseshoes and nails for use in his trade. He used the same two anvils for fifty years.

John F. Buyce's reputation as an expert blacksmith spread.

People insisted there was no better smithy between Northville and Utica. He was one of the first to use "corrective shoeing." Often-times, when the hoof was punctured, he provided a sterile dressing by first packing the wound with tar and a preparation known as oakum, on top of which was laid a protective leather covering to fit under the shoe.

John had a way of dealing with sulky horses, too. The most unruly animals would find themselves raised from the floor in an ox-frame built with pulleys and suspended with straps from the ceiling, despite the fact that many of the horses used in lumbering weighed at least a ton. The horse's foot would then be pulled back and strapped through a ring, where it stayed in position until the job was done. The shoeing of lumbermen's horses and those used to pull the daily tallyho stage comprised the greater part of the business. John's brother, Alvah, joined him in the work around 1904.

Accommodating the picturesque stage formed a rigid routine. Both teams were shod in darkness—the first on arrival from Northville at 7 o'clock at night, the second between 5 and 7 o'clock in the morning before the return trip was made. John F. could be depended upon to be on hand as required. The irrepressible Pants Lawrence used to remark that Buyce was so regular in his arrivals at the shop that he would use the same tracks throughout the entire winter and, as the weather warmed and cooled, the tracks would freeze solid. Then every spring when the snow went off, Pants would have to get out there in the road and chop off the snow posts that were John Buyce's footprints.

By 1920, horse-drawn vehicles were in curtailed use and the Buyces centered much of their attention on wood-working and the metal trades. Ever since Fitch Buyce had conceived the design of the Lake Pleasant rowboat, John F. had had a hankering to devote more attention to its perfection. The advice of his father continued to ring in his ears.

"If you'll change it in a few places, John, I believe it will make a good boat," the aging carpenter had said.

In his earliest days of boat-building, John F. would find a spruce or hemlock tree with a prominent root curved outward. He would dig out the root and take it to Asa Aird's sawmill to be sawed into slabs two inches thick. Later, after extensive lumbering had destroyed the choicest of such roots, flat knees of oak were used.

Buyce made twenty-five of these boats each year, every one painstakingly fashioned by hand. They sold for seventy-five dollars apiece. If one insisted on the luxury of cane seats and mahogany, the price was one hundred and fifteen. The more frail guide boats, weighing only forty-five pounds, were constructed of lighter lumber.

There were only three manufacturers of such boats at the time—John A. Rutan of New York City, Moon of Poland, N.Y., and the Buyces. The Lake Pleasant-produced craft became famous on all lakes in the Adirondacks and were shipped to Canada and eastern seaboard States as far south as Florida, as well. Two or three are still in use on Adirondack lakes.

The light guide boat built for J. Howard Hanson, earliest of the summer residents at Lake Pleasant, is not among them. The brand-new boat was in use on July 4th by rotund John Sturges, who was employed by Hanson as guide and in general work. Young Howard Hanson and Henry Cochrane decided it would be good fun if John were given a surprise. The two stood on the outlet bridge near the Osborne Inn while Sturges rowed underneath. At the appropriate moment, a huge firecracker was dropped into the boat. Harsh words were uttered by a surprised John Sturges when a hole blown in the bottom sent the craft plummeting beneath the waves.

John F.'s ability as a woodworker was further demonstrated when he made the sills of the windows of the new Speculator Methodist Church and cut the altar on his band saw. His accomplishment in intricate metal working is shown in the ornament atop the steeple, a product of his hand forging, and in the huge iron gates on the Market Street entrance to the former

A. V. Morris property in Amsterdam, presently owned by Mr. and Mrs. Herbert L. Shuttleworth, 2nd. Lamps and huge wrought andirons were a specialty.

One bit of planning, left to others, was an object of consternation to John Buyce when the Methodist Church was constructed. A small door gave entrance to the Sunday School room; inside were large swinging doors. Seeing the arrangement, John expressed concern for church funerals. The only way of getting a casket to the altar would be to lift it over the heads of the congregation, it appeared.

His fears were justified. The death of 350-pound John Sturges was the first in the community after the church was dedicated. It was impossible to bring the casket into the sanctuary. Then and there, a double door had to be cut before the funeral could be held.

John F. used to build the old-fashioned three-seated buckboards used for hard riding in the woods, as well as lumber wagons, cutters, sleighs and the bobsters employed for hauling logs in the area's lumbering industry.

Back in the days before the modern power-driven engines, he used to be commissioned by the Town of Lake Pleasant to construct devices for freeing the roads of snow. Huge snow rollers, eight feet high and twelve feet wide, were first built to roll and pack the snow. Later, they were superseded by the large wooden snowplows the Buyces built.

John F. Buyce served his village and township in other ways. Beginning in 1896, he held the office of town clerk for six years. He was supervisor of the town for two five-year terms. For six years he was mayor of Speculator. He was a member of many social and fraternal organizations, including the Masons, Shriners, and the Foresters.

Death came to John F. Buyce in 1947 at the age of seventy-eight. His brother, Alvah, died in 1955, aged eighty-three. Behind them was left a venerable tradition. John F. would have been proud to know that his grandsons are carrying on.

THE TRAGEDY OF EMMA MEAD

THE COMMUNITY would not have been Indian Lake without a few families of full-blooded Indians living within the town. After all, the place had derived its name from the old Abenaki Indian, Sabael Benedict, who had lived on the lake's shores until mid-century, when he was more than a hundred years old.

Sabael left descendants, but they were to be augmented before 1860 by the arrival from Oneida of John and Joe Mitchell and the family of Elijah Camp. Before the turn of the century, Joe Mitchell was killed in an accident on the railroad from Raquette Lake to the main line, and John had said he guessed "two injuns met." The others remained in the town.

Elijah and Elizabeth Camp lived near Indian River for a time, then built the third frame house to be constructed in the village. Of their several children, Gabriel, Samuel and Emma grew to adulthood.

Although the family early assumed the white man's ways, Elizabeth Camp continued to wear native Indian clothing most of the time. Elijah was occupied as guide, ultimately establishing a hunting camp in the wilderness regions of the area.

Emma Mead, born September 11, 1866, grew to a singularly beautiful girl. A favorite of the father, she loved the woods and spent a great deal of her time at Elijah's rustic retreat. Here she met the hunters and fishermen whom her father guided and entertained.

To the camp one day came a handsome young man from the distant cities. His friendly manner appealed immediately to Emma, turned eighteen that year. His urbane ways wove for her a genuine charm.

Gabriel Mead was similarly struck with the Indian girl's unusual beauty and native grace. The young man knew at once that this was the woman he must make his wife.

[142]

Theirs was a rapid courtship that ended with their marriage by Erastus Farrington, local justice of the peace. Then followed days of blissful living born of faithful love.

It was to be short-lived. When Gabe Mead's wealthy and socially-prominent parents learned of the marriage, they were appalled. Indignation mounted as they contemplated a full-blooded Indian as their son's wife. She could never become the mistress of a city home worthy of their son. Social ostracism was assured. And their own association with the rough-hewn Elijah and his buckskin-clad wife as parents-in-law was an incongruous surmise. The whole thing was completely unthinkable. Measures must be taken at once.

Gabe and Emma Mead's happiness paled before the clouds of his family's extreme displeasure. Gabe became morose and took to drink. Emma, who was expecting a child to bless their union, was apprehensive and distressed.

The determination of the Mead Family was not to be outdone. There were turbulent discussions with the newlyweds and with the elder Camps. Feelings were deeply injured and Indian pride gave way to bitterness and defeat.

The Meads went so far as to claim that their son was mentally incompetent, as they struggled to have the marriage annulled. A settlement, whispered as reaching to the sum of ten thousand dollars, was made. Her marriage destroyed, the grieving Emma apathetically accepted. Gabriel Mead left. Some say he returned one time for a clandestine meeting with the young woman he so dearly loved, but it was much the spectacle of a scavenger picking over an irremediable ruin.

Bessie L. Mead was born in July, 1886, a handsome baby whom her saddened mother adored. Emma purchased a larger home for her parents on a beautiful hilltop setting with an unsurpassed view south of the village. She opened a small store at Indian Lake.

The young Bessie developed into a beautiful child. Emma loved her companionship and frequently took her daughter with her to the store.

It was a beautiful warm day in late February. Outside, the three-year-old Bessie played on the porch in the warm winter sun and exhilarating mountain air while her mother served a customer inside. No one saw the little child crawl slowly onto the porch railing until it was too late. With a terrified scream, the hapless youngster plunged to the ground. Badly injured, she soon passed away.

The heart-broken Emma lived alone with her mother at Indian Lake for the remainder of her life. It was perhaps her bitterness that prevented remarriage. Always, she dwelt with quiet dignity in the shadows of the early cataclysm that marked her dismal life.

Emma Camp Mead died on December 4, 1934 at the age of sixty-eight, to be buried in the village cemetery beside the small body of her beloved little daughter. "A tragic life" is the pronouncement of former neighbors at Indian Lake.

ALL ABOUT BEARS

THERE WAS keen interest on the part of both Albert and Ortie Dunning when Perry Page, the hermit of Mud Lake, brought a live bear to their Speculator hotel. Bears, they knew, could prove quite an attraction, as long as they were kept on the end of a stout rope and not allowed to run wild.

The Dunning brothers decided to go halves on the cost. Perry Page left the wealthier for his woodland retreat. Albert and Ortie became the proud possessors of an untamed bear.

All was well until the novelty wore thin and care of the animal became an ever-increasing burden. As the days passed, Albert grew something less than enthusiastic with the pet. Ortie's continued interest in bruin only made the burden more difficult.

Annoyances were compounded as hotel business took Ortie

The Covered Bridge, Wells, built in 1866. Nathaniel Cowles helped frame the structure on the flats back of Burnham's store.

Tally-ho Stage at Hosley's Hotel, Wells, where passengers were fed and horses changed on the Northville-Lake Pleasant run.

Commercial Hotel, Indian Lake, a stopping place on the stage route from North Creek to Blue Mountain Lake.

Indian River Hotel, run for years by John Sault on the site where the Indian Lake people first settled.

on an overnight visit to the city. Albert flatly rebelled at becoming sole nursemaid to the creature while his brother was away. The two finally agreed it would be easier on Albert if the bear were tied in the cellar of the hotel.

The following evening, Ortie alighted from the Northville stage and walked into the hotel, his trip completed. He was filled with news of his travels. Suddenly, he broke off in mid-sentence to inquire about their ferocious pet.

"The fool thing howled all night," cried the disdainful Albert. "About 3 o'clock, I got up and went down cellar. There was no other way. I knocked my half in the head with the axe, and your half died."

*   *   *   *   *

When John Wadsworth appeared in the doorway of the saloon at Wells that warm spring day, bartender and barroom loungers took one look, emitted frantic yells, and ran for the nearest exit. Not that there was anything about John's appearance to inspire terror. He and his family had lived up on the Windfall back of Wells for many years and were well-known thereabouts. Nor was John's conduct anything to cause apprehension. It was merely some of the interests he had.

It had all started the previous summer when the smiling John had gone, with shining pail, over next to the Windfall woods to pick raspberries. It was a pleasant summer day and he was intent in his work, gathering the ripe red fruit beside a large old tree that had crashed to earth in a recent storm.

As he rounded the upturned stump of the tree, the old huntsman was surprised to come upon two little bear cubs romping near the scraggly roots. John could not resist taking one affectionately into his arms.

Just at that moment, the perplexed, half-angered mother bear appeared. John was caught red-handed. Surely, though unwittingly, he had given any decent, law-abiding parent cause for rage.

As the bear approached, Wadsworth crawled onto the long

dark tree trunk, the cub still in his arms. The mother bear followed on the ground.

Hastily, the hunter doffed his wide-brimmed hat and flailed at the huge, lumbering beast.

"Flee, you feather-foot!" he commanded, and the astonished animal gave momentary pause.

John ran the length of the fallen tree as fast as he could.

"William!" he called to his son in a voice that could be heard to Northville. "William, come out here quick!"

William had no time to reach the scene before his father, complete with bear cub, had reached the safety of their small, unpainted house. Strangely, the mother bear had wandered slowly back into the woods.

A few days later, John brought his new-found pet triumphantly into Wells village. Dan Cochrane, the hotelman, felt he could use the animal as an added attraction for his guests. A deal was made.

Late fall neared and the last city sportsman headed back down the mountain roads. Dan Cochrane realized that the bear would want to hibernate for the winter. A suitable place was made for the animal to hole up.

Candlemas Day approached—the day when, according to mountain tradition, bears come temporarily out of hibernation. If they see their shadow, six weeks of cold winter weather will follow. If not, the winter will shortly conclude.

The day was partly cloudy. Anxious to do his part to help speed winter on its way, the burly hotelman waited for an overcast spell of suitable length, then went out and tugged on the bear's ample chain. The indifferent bruin proved uncooperative. Resentful of the impertinent intrusion, it merely growled and snarled and fell instantly back into blissful sleep.

When the pet emerged in the spring, it had grown both big and ugly. Visitors to its den were content to give it wide berth.

The day came when John Wadsworth paid a visit to the village, stopping for some time at the local saloon. The more John drank, the warmer his heart became. He figured maybe he would pay a visit to his untamed, fretting friend. Warned to keep his distance from the animal, the hunter merely snorted. Who was afraid of a bear?

Some minutes later, the teetering John reappeared in the doorway of the establishment. Around his shoulders was draped the snapping, snarling, recently-awakened bear. It was this that caused such overwhelming consternation. The bar was emptied of bartender and customers in record time.

FOLKS AT INDIAN LAKE

SIMULTANEOUS OPERATION of two divergent businesses could keep a man busy. John Sault's joint proprietorship of the Indian River Hotel and the grocery at Indian Lake Village was no exception to the rule.

John could never read nor write. Instead, he kept records that were a fine combination of hieroglyphics and hasty cartoon, records that frequently bore resemblance to the paintings of the aboriginal Indians who roamed the land years before.

John greeted one of his customers rather firmly one day with the direct remark:

"When are you going to pay me for that head of cheese you bought?"

The customer looked startled.

"Why, John, I didn't buy any cheese from you." He hesitated. "But let me see now, I did buy a grindstone."

Sometimes, John Sault could not read his own cartoons.

Into John's store one day strode an Indian Lake neighbor who wanted to buy his son a jacket but could not recall the size. The storekeeper asked if his customer knew the young man's height.

"He's a big, strapping boy," the villager replied. "Let's see, he's either five feet nine inches or nine feet five inches. I don't right know which."

It was about this time that the baseball fans of Indian Lake had begun to worry about their team's chances in the mountain village league. They couldn't seem to find a catcher worthy of their nine.

The whimsical blacksmith, George Tripp, thought he had an answer.

"You should try to get Jack Ducket," he told the troubled sports followers, "because he's the only man I know of who has ever caught a lightning ball. It was like this: Jack bought a new stove and attached a hot water pipe. He had just left the house when a thunderstorm began to rumble and roll in the mountains. Jack was just outside the door when there was a sharp flash, an awful roar, and a bolt of lightning headed right for the water pipe on the new stove. Jack didn't wait. He lunged through that door and into the kitchen. And he grabbed that lightning ball before it ever hit that stove."

There was also Prent Brown, who killed a muskrat, only to see the dead carcass float away down the river before he could reach it. So, the next muskrat he saw, more rapid tactics were required.

As the muskrat climbed to the top of a rock, Prent fired at the creature, threw his gun behind him, and leaped to the rock. To his surprise, his hands closed on a live and wriggling animal.

Prent learned why. At that moment, the charge of shot from his own gun struck him full in the seat of the pants.

RETURN OF THE "BUTTERCUP"

DURING THE SUMMER OF 1959, George Boudreau and Frank McIntyre, local amateur skin-divers, made a remarkable discovery on the floor of Long Lake. Lying in eighteen feet of water about 500 feet off the Sagamore Hotel dock, lay a passenger steamboat, twenty-five feet long and seven feet wide. It took a lot of doing, but by September 12th they had managed to raise the craft to the surface and give it earth-bound harbor in Ed Wilson's garage at the Deerland corners.

Old-timers were consulted. "Yes," said the venerable Ike Robinson, now in his ninetieth year. "It was most certainly the old 'Buttercup.'" He was the only living person who had sailed in the steamer back when he was fourteen years of age. The boat had laid in its watery grave, lost and forgotten, for some seventy-odd years.

Like much of the modern heritage of the Central Adirondacks, the virtually unremembered story of the "Buttercup" began with William West Durant, whose deep interest in the mountains knew few bounds. Development here must begin on a grand scale, he decided, when he visited the lake country in the 1870's.

Durant's enthusiasm stemmed both from his own love of the mountains and his business interests. Successor to his father as president of the Adirondack Railroad from Saratoga to North Creek, he early became aware that promoting travel deeper into the wilderness would only further his financial goals.

In rapid succession, he constructed in 1877 his own lavish year-around resort home, Camp Pine Knot, on Long Point in Raquette Lake, and built three additional luxurious properties which he sold to J. Pierpont Morgan, Alfred G. Vanderbilt, and Governor Timothy L. Woodruff. He raised and contributed money to build St. Hubert's Episcopal Church; for

the Catholics, he built St. William's. He constructed a golf
course on Eagle Lake near the site of Ned Buntline's old log
cabin, established the first post office in 1889 at Raquette Lake,
and organized the Adirondack, Lake George & Saratoga Telegraph Company.

The key to it all was transportation, the railroad man knew.
In 1877, he established a line of four and six-horse Concord
coaches from the railroad terminus at North Creek to Blue
Mountain Lake, a distance of thirty miles. A line of rowboats
carried passengers the additional twelve miles to Raquette Lake.
Gradually, steamboat transportation was added. Tourists began to flock to the area.

Now came a more ambitious scheme to extend travel by boat
into Long Lake and on toward Saranac. There would be diffi-
culties. The level of the lake would have to be raised. But the
rewards in the influx of money-spending city visitors would
be of such obvious benefit that no one could fail to recognize
its value.

Durant's own fervor was so great, he failed to recognize that
it might not always be shared by others. He was reckoning
without the wishes of the Long Lake people themselves.

With the high-handed methods of the expert promoter,
Durant met with the town fathers, explained his plan and announced that a carry would be required from Forked Lake to
Long Lake. An expenditure of one thousand dollars by the
town would amply cover construction costs. There was no
thought in his mind that Supervisor Robert Shaw, Town Clerk
O. E. Boyden and the other members of the board might not
be thoroughly convinced.

At the annual town meeting of March 16, 1886, the talk
was of little else. The dam being built by Durant would de-
stroy much of the lake's beauty. Beaches would be submerged
and trees destroyed. The guides—and that included just about
every able-bodied man in the community—were particularly
outraged. Bringing people by modern transportation to the far

reaches of the lake would make much of their own work un-
necessary. Badly needed income would be impaired. The tax-
payers saw no justification for any such expenditure of their
hard-earned money. For whatever acquiescence they might
have made, the town fathers stood accused.

Justly indignant, Supervisor Shaw rose with a determined
motion: "Resolved that the appropriation of one thousand
dollars to be expended by W. W. Durant in building a carry
from Forked Lake to Long Lake is without authority, illegal
and partisan—that it is the sense of this town, expressed in open
town meeting . . . that the said appropriation be suppressed
and the whole transaction be disapproved." The measure was
passed unanimously. Only one other item of business was trans-
acted—a ten-dollar bounty on bears was reaffirmed.

Completely undaunted, William West Durant went ahead
with his plans. Down near Buttermilk Falls, he built his dam.
The twenty-five-foot boat, the "Buttercup," was brought by
sled in winter to become the first steamboat to ply Long Lake.

Damaged feelings were scarcely soothed. The shores of the
lake and even some of the summer homes were flooded. At the
property of the Rev. Dr. Joseph Duryea, the camp location became an island instead of a peninsula. The trees lining the
shores began to lose their leaves and turn gray. And the guides
claimed that the pinch was on.

Aware of the discontent, Durant kept two men watching the
dam in alternating shifts. The "Buttercup" was kept secure at
its dock at the original Sagamore Hotel. For at least a year, the
boat made its daily trip from David Helms' hotel to the carry
at Raquette Falls.

One night, as the guard sat before his campfire at the dam, a
bullet suddenly struck the embers. Without waiting, the guard
set out for his room at Johnson's Lodge, two miles below the
falls. On his way, he heard a tremendous blast of dynamite as
the dam was blown. The next morning, it was discovered that
the "Buttercup" had totally vanished.

The ominous silence was never broken. No one ever knew

the responsible parties. It was fully ten years before another steamboat was in operation on Long Lake.

The "Buttercup" was found remarkably preserved after its long years of submersion, its steam boilers and brass fittings virtually intact. The wooden sides remained firm; only a large tell-tale hole in one side spoke of the boat's untimely demise. Of the several tools that were found, one bore the meaningful initials "W.D."

DEAN OF THE GUIDES

PROBABLY no name is more closely associated with the Southern Adirondack region than that of Lawrence. It was from the land-owning Lawrences of New York City that many of the earliest settlers of the area acquired their acreage. It is from descendants of these New York land-holders that many have gained even richer reward. The earlier Lawrences conveyed land; the later Lawrences conveyed lore. Some of the most memorable experiences of a host of Adirondack visitors are attributable to these ample woodsmen and capable guides.

When Marinus Lawrence first came to the mountains with Peter, his father, in 1846, he brought with him a love for woodsmanship and hunting that was the heritage of his fine old American stock. He called himself a farmer, and farmer he was; but like so many of his neighbors, he was happiest when he was tramping the woodland trails. And after he had married James Scidmore's daughter, Phoebe, and they had raised their family of five sons and three daughters, that same inheritance had been passed to each of the boys.

All five were guides at various times, as adept at dealing with demanding sportsmen as at scaring up elusive woodland game. And the Lawrence hunting camp at Pillsbury Lake, so ably run for so many years by Sam and Elizabeth Satterlee Lawrence, is still in the family's hands.

But probably none is more widely known for preserving the traditions of the Adirondacks than Frank A. Lawrence, fourth of Marinus' and Phoebe's sons.

It was because of his relative position in the family that Frank early derived the familiar nickname by which he was always best known. The mountains provided but meager living for a growing family and clothes were remade and frugally handed down. Economy further demanded an eye to the future for the needs of a developing lad. So young "Pants," in over-sized trousers made over from his father's or passed down from his older brothers, got his name.

"Pants" early grew to have a commanding appearance. He was a big-boned man, six feet, three inches tall, with large hands and feet. Exceptionally well-built, in appearance he was something of that of a red-cheeked forest nimrod. His booming voice had an engaging quality. He liked people and enjoyed talking with them. His innate affection was returned many-fold.

Perhaps the best known person in the Lake Pleasant area, Pants endeared himself to the summer people, for whom he was as much a part of the community as the mountains or the island in the lake. He was assuredly the resort's unofficial ambassador.

One day, he was sitting on the porch of Robb Stuart's store when some guests of the Osborne Inn strolled by. Recognizing Pants, they stopped, greeted him cordially by name, and engaged him in conversation.

Pants responded in kind. It was a warm-hearted meeting of old friends. With hearty farewells, the summer visitors moved slowly up the road. Pants turned to the storekeeper in the doorway of the grocery.

"Who them g—— d—— lamplighters?" he asked. "You know? I don't."

As a guide, Pants never wasted words. Off duty, he could often become loquacious, especially after a drink or two. Not that he was a drinker. He always limited himself to enough to float a ship, he said, but felt, as he grew older, he would have to give up because they kept building the ships bigger and bigger.

As a guide, he was a natural. He knew all the streams where fish abounded and all the runways frequented by the deer. And at night, over the campfire, he had an inexhaustible fund of stories that kept sportsmen listening when sound judgment and tired bodies told them it was long past time to bed down for the night.

Much in demand by sportsmen, he met hundreds of people, many of them as prominent in their chosen professions as Pants was adept in his. When the State of New York began licensing guides, he was Guide No. 1. He won another distinction, too. For years, behind the bar at Osborne's Inn, was a framed plaque testifying to his ability as a story-teller. Pants held the No. 1 "Adirondack Liar's License," the bold print affirmed.

Tall tales were Pants' specialty. To each huntsman, he told a different story. Of the hundreds of sportsmen he met, each recalls one or more stories recounted by Pants with no resemblance to that told to others. They were offered in utter seriousness and as Gospel truth. Everyone felt that the element of fact, based on his own experiences, was somehow inherent in each.

Very often, guests at Osborne's Inn used to comment about the fine pine paneling in the bar. Pants always called it hickory. And when people asked how they got such exceptional hickory paneling, Pants had the answer.

"It came about a few years back that I was logging up Whitaker Lake way. I was kinda late getting out of the woods one day. And you know how it is when you're late and anxious to get home; you hurry a little. So the team was jogging down the trail road, and the empty wagon was jouncing around, with me holding on every way I could. It was one of those nice days, the first real warm day of spring, and the snow was all gone, except in the northeast hollows. It was so warm that I druv all the way home that evening in nothing but my red underwear.

"Just as I pulled around the last bend before you get to the flats, I slowed up the team a little before they hit the flat rocks that go clear across the trail. And it was a good thing I did, too, 'cause there, spang in the middle of that big warm rock, I see coiled the biggest rattler I ever seed, with his rattles aringin', all ready to strike.* I yanked back on the lines and the horses reared up, the sparks aflyin' from the shoes on the rock.

"I saw the rattler strike, and quick as I could get the team stopped, I jumped down and run around to hold their heads and see which horses would have to be shot. But you know what I seed when I got there?

"That snake had missed both horses, and had struck that wagon-tongue right back of the yoke. It had hit so hard that its fangs were in clear to the back of the jaw. Its tail was aslashin' every which way, but I finally grabbed onto it and, pull as hard as I would, I couldn't jerk it loose. I finally had to take out my hand axe and chop off its head.

"Well, I saved the rattles, gentled the horses, finally got going, and pulled into the mill yard just about dark. I unhooked the team and tied up in the stable, and hung up the harness ready to go the next morning.

"Well, you know, the next morning, it wasn't light yet when I got out to hook up the team. I led them out into the yard where I had left the wagon, and backed them over the tongue, and tried to get the yoke to fit. But I fumbled around there in the dark and couldn't get the tongue to go into the ring. So, ruther than fool around any more, I just led the team over to the spare wagon and drove into the woods.

"A couple of times that day I looked at the yoke, thought

* Pants' story is particularly unusual in view of the fact that the Adirondacks have never been known to harbor a poisonous snake of any kind.

maybe the ring was bent or broke, but I didn't see that it was. So, that night while I was goin' home, I got to thinkin' why it was I couldn't get the ring of that neck-yoke to fit over that wagon-tongue.

"So, when I got down to the mill yard and unhooked the team, I went back and looked at that wagon I had druv the day before. And you know what? That wagon tongue that was always three inches at the tip was now about a foot across. I couldn't figure that out, but I was tired and I just went on in to bed.

"The next morning, after I had made my first trip, I got thinkin' again, so I stopped at the yard and took a look at that tongue in the full light of day. And you know what? That hickory tongue was now a log better than a foot across. So I hooked onto it and took it over to the mill and got it sawed into half-inch panel strips, and them's the pieces we used to panel this here barroom wall.

"And you know, every spring, when the snow is gone except for the northeast hollows, a little bit of snake oil comes oozin' out of that hickory panel, and the hired girl gives it a wipe or two with lamb's wool, and it has a polish as good as a looking glass."

Asked his occupation from 1890 to 1908, Pants would tell you he was a laborer. But later occupation forced him to abandon the term. Although twice-married, there were never any children to share his glory. After all, there could only be one Pants Lawrence.

For a time, the mountain resident and his first wife, Hattie, ran that small inn known as the Speculator House. John Conover of Amsterdam paid a visit to the bar one evening for a chat with the landlord. John had been there only a short time when Pants asked him to tend bar while he attended to some important business at hand.

Pants was absent for perhaps a half-hour. His booming voice was heard in animated conversation near the lobby door. A feminine voice indicated that his wife was a party to the melee.

When he returned, Pants and his wife had unmistakably gone their separate ways. His first marriage had reached its close.

It was prior to 1915 that Pants was nominated for the office of sheriff of Hamilton County. Printed cards were forthwith issued bearing the illustration of a pair of trousers on a clothesline. Below was the simple message: "Vote for Pants." Thanks perhaps to the cards and, in greater measure, to Pants' vivid personality, the campaign was a success. Pants proudly wore a checkered vest with a heavy gold watch chain as he fulfilled the duties of leading law-enforcement officer.

The lean, ramrod-straight man was to be seen everywhere.

Pants' brother-in-law, Lee L. Fountain, ran the Whitehouse for a time in Speculator. It was an inn that attracted many summer visitors, who used to eat their noon-day meal in the large, cool dining room and then wander out onto the porch. There they would often find Pants sitting on the steps, his back against the rail post, gazing off across the mountains.

Almost invariably, their first remark would be about how delightfully cool the temperature was in the Whitehouse dining room.

"Why is it?" They would want to know.

After several had asked, Pants would explain.

"Well, it's this way," he would relate. "Up the west branch of the Sacandaga, there whips up some powerful winds in the winter, and as these winds wind up the mountain to Mud Lake Notch, they are for sure cyclones.

"Now, since there ain't much going on around Speculator in the winter time, we decided last year to go up there with two barrels of old molasses and paste it on both sides of the Notch just ahead of a blow. When the high winds got up the river, they hit the Notch, slowed down some, and then got stuck there. Then two of the boys and me went up there and, with the long cross-cut, in one day we sawed off enough of that cyclone to fill the ice house. And now, in the summer time, all they have to do is chip off a chunk and hang it in the doorway of the dining room to keep it right cool."

When, during several summers, raging forest fires were threatening the woodlands, speculation as to their cause and prevention was rife. Pants had his own explanation. The fires were caused by the slub dub with the sandpaper tail, he said. And every time those slub dubs would run over the fox-fire stumps, they'd start those old forests blazing.

Pants it was who sent a hound after a deer up Jessup's River and put that all-fired deer straight into Puget Sound.

He used to tell about the time they had that contest at Speculator to determine the ugliest man. Aaron Arnold, with his dark whiskers and small nose, had suffered a stroke that had left an eyelid pulled far down. Arnold was Pants' candidate.

"I want you to go in there and look as natural as you can," Pants instructed him. Of course, as Pants told it, Aaron Arnold was the winner by a mile.

One day, the old guide stormed into the local drug store at Speculator. "I want some of the g—— damnedest, harshest cough syrup you've got in the place," he averred.

The next customer was less bombastic.

"You suppose they got any of the coffin medicine in here?" he wanted to know.

Pants liked to hang out at the local hotels. When Pugilist Gene Tunney arrived to make the Osborne Inn his head-quarters while training for his first fight with Heavyweight Champion Jack Dempsey, the old guide was right on hand to extend the community's warmest welcome. Bill Osborne would commission Pants to take Tunney on hikes to Elm Lake and similar distances to get him away from the enervating fanfare and ever-present crowds.

"He increased my knowledge of woodcraft considerably," Tunney said.

Gene and Pants became fast friends. Tunney called Pants one of his most loyal followers and a faithful daily attendant at the practice ring. Gene saw to it that Pants attended each of his fights. They were the woodsman's first trips outside the mountains.

Pants Lawrence lived to a ripe old age, well beyond his eightieth year, but illness troubled his final days, causing the old woodsman to be sent to a nursing home in Gloversville and finally to a hospital in Utica. Friends, including Gene Tunney, rallied to his financial assistance in those unhappy years.

Finally, death came to the hospitalized Pants Lawrence. His second wife, Katherine, was living in Connecticut at the time. Asked about the disposition of his body, she refused to allow its removal to his mountain homeland. Pants was buried on the Utica hospital grounds.

The information was received with shock and sorrow among the old guide's many friends in the Town of Lake Pleasant. Several offered to pay the cost of reburial in the Speculator Cemetery, where they felt Pants Lawrence rightfully belonged. Among them was Gene Tunney. But permission could not be gained. Pants Lawrence of Lake Pleasant had left the mountains to stay.

Yet death could not dull the vivid memory and proud heritage he had left behind. The name of Pants Lawrence and the stories he told assume renewed vitality in widespread places throughout the country where former visitors to the Southern Adirondacks meet. And, in Lake Pleasant country, the memory of the finest of guides and ablest of men remains wholesomely alive as a model for present-day woodsmen. In the finest of American tradition, Pants Lawrence's contribution to the Adirondack region was great.

EMILY STEVENS' WISH

FEW ADIRONDACK GUIDES could ever boast of the wide range of experiences that came to the veteran woodsman, Frank "Pants" Lawrence. Pants' way of describing his adventures gave them such additional color as to forestall duplication by lesser men, no matter how hard they tried.

There was one experience in Pants Lawrence's life that, with his love for his fellow men, impressed him greatly. Nor was embellishment of the facts necessary in the retelling. He used to dwell on it from time to time as his last years were at hand.

It concerned the golden-haired, strikingly fair Emily Stevens, cousin of the prominent actress, Minnie Maddern Fiske, and a famous actress in her own right.

Older than her cousin by some sixteen years, Minnie Maddern Fiske had achieved stardom in New York in 1881 at the age of sixteen. At the turn of the century, when Emily Stevens was twenty, she appeared with Mrs. Fiske in such well-known Broadway productions as "Mary of Magdala," "Becky Sharpe," and "Hedda Gabler." Then she left her older cousin to play with George Arliss in "The Devil" in 1908 and "Septimus" in 1909. But Emily Stevens' method of acting had been shaped by her cousin and at times her voice was known to echo startlingly that of the older player.

Minnie Maddern Fiske acquired an early love for the Adirondacks, and came to Lake Pleasant at the height of her stage career. On December 21, 1900, her husband, Harrison Grey Fiske of New York City, acquired twelve acres of land west of Lake Pleasant Village from John and Laura Pelcher. This land he transferred to his wife on March 12, 1904. Three years later, Minnie Maddern Fiske transferred the land to Mary Potter Phillips of New York and Ethel P. Cunningham of

Pants Lawrence and Emily Stevens. Pants felt badly when the famous actress committed suicide in New York in 1928.

Sturges House, Speculator, a haven for city sportsmen for eighty-seven years.

Outlet of Lake Pleasant around 1880, years before the present public beach was begun.

Toles Satterlee's Store, Newton's Corners, where from 1870, handmade shingles were bartered for household staples.

Philadelphia, and proceeded to make her summer home at Big Moose near Old Forge in Herkimer County.

Her beautiful and personable cousin, Emily Stevens, with an equal affection for the mountains, chose Lake Pleasant. On one of her earliest trips to the area, she camped along the beautiful sand beach at the foot of the lake, on land later acquired—perhaps unknowingly, in view of his aversion to the theatre—by "Pop" Tibbitts for his Camp-of-the-Woods. Later, she stayed at the Morley Hotel in Lake Pleasant Village and at the summer residence of Mrs. H. V. N. Phillips nearby.

Finally, on March 9, 1917, Emily Stevens purchased beautiful "Pine Point," a plot of fifty acres, on the far side of Sacandaga Lake, that had been surrendered in bankruptcy by Harrison Grey Fiske. For five years, she occupied the property, the sole access to which was by boat across the entire width of the lake. On May 9, 1922, the summer place was sold to Edgar Call. It was later acquired by the late Arthur Shuttleworth, president of Mohawk Carpet Mills, and is now occupied by his son, Herbert L. Shuttleworth, 2nd, president of Mohasco Industries, and his family.

As witty and urbane in real life as the roles she portrayed on the stage, Emily Stevens had a mind of her own. Pants Lawrence, as sheriff, first came to know her when, having crossed the lake by boat from her summer home, she refused to dress at the hotel, preferring the privacy of the county jail. Pants was both sympathetic and amused.

Emily Stevens went on to score in the New York theatre. In 1924, she was acclaimed in the role of Mathilde Fay in the Theater Guild production of "Fata Morgana," at the Garrick Theatre in New York City. The following season, she achieved success in "Mahroupoulos' Secret," a play based on the legend of the woman of eternal youth. Meanwhile, she continued to visit the Adirondacks.

One day, when Pants dropped in for a visit to the Phillips' summer home, where Miss Stevens was a guest, he learned of a plan to plant three trees in a row just below the house.

"And when we die, the three of us are to be buried beneath them," Pants was told, "the Phillipses at each end and Emily in the middle."

The trees were planted and, as time passed, they grew to substantial size.

One dark day, ominous word reached Pants Lawrence. A depressed Emily Stevens, without a major stage role for a year, had committed suicide in her large suite at the Great Northern Hotel in New York City on January 2, 1928 at the age of forty-six. She had never married and no immediate relatives were at hand. No note was found. She was buried in New York City.

Some time after the funeral, a note was discovered underneath the draperies of Emily Stevens' apartment. It was addressed to "Dear Robert."

"I hope you find this note," it said. "Because of this terrible act, I want my body cremated." Emily Stevens' message further specified that her ashes were to be sent to Sheriff Frank "Pants" Lawrence to be buried under the tree in the Phillips' yard at Lake Pleasant.

The message had come too late. It was the deepest regret of the old guide's life.

THE POND LILY GUIDE

EVEN THE Number One Guide of the Adirondacks occasionally had to have his license renewed. Pants Lawrence went over to Woodrow Call's house in Lake Pleasant Village to procure the necessary credential. As he did so, he was conscious of the fact that, in recent years, so many of the summer people were seeking his services to take them on picnics to nearby places. It wasn't like the old days at all.

Pants' brisk rap on the door was answered by Mrs. Call, a

graduate of Syracuse University and a newcomer to the community. Woodrow was not at home.

Pants stated his purpose and Mrs. Call had a question.

"Are you a guide?" she wanted to know.

As usual, the indefatigable Pants was ready with an answer. "I'm not a full-fledged guide," he informed her seriously. "Matter of fact, I'm just a pond-lily guide. I guide women mostly. I take people downstream on picnics and they pick pond lilies."

Pants got his license and a new name as well. The foremost guide of the Adirondacks was henceforth laughingly labeled "the pond-lily guide."

Pants' conversation with Mrs. Charles Nisbet did much to further his nickname. He was seated on the porch of the Brooks Hotel when the early summer resident came strolling up the plank sidewalk toward the village center.

Seeing the veteran guide, Mrs. Nisbet paused thoughtfully. "I'm looking for someone who wants to work," she told him. "No one seems to want to."

"I'd work," replied the tall, broad-shouldered Pants brightly. "I can't do heavy work, though. I'd need help to get a cake of ice out of the ice house. I ain't too particular though, because I've got a hunting party coming this fall."

Mrs. Nisbet sighed unhappily as, wordlessly, she resumed her walk toward the general store. You couldn't find a man who wanted to work.

THAT WAS A DEER

THERE WAS the usual large mounted deerhead on the wall of the lobby when the old guide, Pants Lawrence, ran the Speculator House. Spying the trophy, a gushing, middle-aged feminine guest of the establishment turned fervent eyes to the proprietor of the hotel.

"That's the most beautiful deerhead I've ever seen!" she exulted. "Tell me, Mr. Lawrence, how did you ever shoot him?"

Surprised perhaps at being called Mr. Lawrence, Pants turned earnest face to his admirer.

"I didn't," Pants drawled. "I was out on Lake Pleasant fishing for trout one June when I heard a crashing in the underbrush, and there stood a fine big buck—and me with no gun. Well, just as I looked, the deer turned. It was black-fly season and the bugs were biting bad. I quickly grabbed my flit gun and shot that old critter with it right under the tail."

The woman was all ears. "And did it kill him?" she inquired breathlessly.

"Well, no," Pants admitted. "But it itched some and he backed up against a tree. And when he finished scratching himself, all that was left was what you see hanging there over the mantel."

THE OSBORNES COME TO TOWN

THE CALENDAR read 1896 when Will Osborne brought his young family to the village of Newton's Corners. Will was a hotel man, as his father had been before him. For a time, he had operated the Broadalbin Hotel in Fulton County. His cousin, Charles, too, had built and operated the Old Orchard Inn in the Town of Northampton at the base of the Adirondacks on Sacandaga Park road.

The Osbornes were of an old family in the Town of Northampton. Grandfather William Osborne, born in 1803, had been a teamster there for many years after coming to settle from Rensselaer County. His son, Hiram, born in 1838, had operated a hotel for some years over at Osborne's Bridge.

Tragedy had a way of stalking the Osbornes. As the Gloversville newspaper told it in its daily issue of February 2, 1894:

"As the result of a petty dispute, a human life was sacrificed Tuesday afternoon in the village of Northampton, this county. The man was Hiram Osborn, the proprietor of the Osborn House, and the slayer was Walter Brown, proprietor of the Fish House.

"The two men were rivals in business, their hotels being on opposite corners of the same street. Unfortunately, they were more than rivals. Since last summer, they were on anything but friendly terms owing to a damaging story which the guest of one hotel circulated about the proprietor of the other.

"Tuesday it had snowed the greater portion of the day and the wind had piled the fleecy particles in drifts upon the streets and sidewalks. The landlord of the Osborn House cleared his sidewalk and his side of the street of snow and piled it in a high ridge. Mr. Brown took offense at this, but no action was taken until one of the drivers, Albert Brownell, drove up to the Osborn House and partly leveled the piled-up snow.

"Mr. Osborn remonstrated with him. Thereupon Brown, seizing a shot gun, mounted the sleigh and directed Brownell to drive through the snow piled up by Osborn. The latter disputed the right of way and tried to turn the horses back, while his son, John, stood nearby with a revolver in his hand.

"The dispute was brief. The inflamed Brown raised the gun and lodged a full charge of bird-shot in the neck and face of Osborn. The latter staggered and fell lifeless to the ground.

"The slayer turned and re-entered his hotel. The frightful tragedy which a speck of reason would have averted, was accomplished. The body of Mr. Osborn was taken into the hotel where the horrified family and spectators stood speechless over the ghastly sight. The neck and side of the face where the shot entered were badly disfigured.

"After the shooting, the wildest excitement spread through the village and the tragedy and its cause were everywhere discussed. Meantime, Brown continued his business for some time after the shooting and then driving to Northville, surrendered to the authorities. He refuses to speak of the occurrence but has retained able lawyers to defend his own life.

"The victim, Hiram Osborn, leaves a wife and four children. For twenty years he has kept a hotel at Northampton and had the reputation of being an obliging and well conducted person. One of his sons, William, conducts a hotel at Broadalbin. Brown has only been in Northville a year. Like Osborn, he has borne a good reputation and people at first refused to believe that he could have been guilty of shooting his rival. He has a wife and two children."

A year later, the Osborne Hotel was destroyed by fire.

Then, as Sportswriter Bill Cunningham once told in his newspaper column, the Osbornes migrated to Newton's Corners under orders from the family physician. "The mother was growing pale and thin. The doctor prescribed the bracing air of the mountains—any mountains—so they had hitched up and driven as far north as there were any roads, and when they stopped at the furthest possible point on the road that they had taken, they were several days from civilization across a couple of ranges, and the name of the place was Speculator."

Bill Cunningham was only partly correct. The name of Newton's Corners was changed to Speculator only through the influence of the Osbornes, who felt that the original name was too rural in nature to permit successful exploitation as a resort center.

Will and Nora Osborne bought and operated the Wilber Hotel in Speculator for a time. Nora ran the hotel laundry. One day the laundry caught fire and the hotel was burned to the ground.

It was a bitter blow that could have thrown a less substantial man out of business for good. But Will Osborne rented and operated the old Adirondack Hotel for a time. Before he was finished, he had built two new hotels.

One was on the main road back from the lake shore. This he rented for a time to the Lawlers. The other was in a prime location between the lake shore and the main road, just south of the outlet, its ample verandas virtually overhanging the lake. This latter hotel was built in 1901. The family moved into the handsome new establishment on April 28, 1902.

Meantime, Osborne had been instrumental in promoting entertainment for the summer visitors. Prior to building his inn, he and Isaiah Perkins had brought an excursion boat from Lake George, transporting it the many miles to Lake Pleasant on sleighs during the winter. It was anchored near the inn that summer with Tom and Lewis Slack as pilots to take sightseers around the lake. It was Osborne and Perkins who also operated the popular dance platform in the grove at the foot of the lake.

Will Osborne had run his new Osborne Inn for one season, when tragedy struck once more. On September 14, 1902, he died at the age of thirty-seven years of septicaemia. Nora Osborne was left to operate the hotel while raising her young family of three—William age ten, Pamelia J., eight, and Robert F., six.

Nora Osborne accepted the challenge and, to her everlasting

credit, caused the Osborne Inn to prosper and her sons to become leading citizens of the town. Then, as the boys became older, she let them take a hand. By 1915, William, then 23, was proprietor of the hotel. His younger brother, Robert, then 18, was chauffeur for the guests. Each year the business grew until it became one of the best-known hostelries in the area.

The original Osborne Inn remains the principal hotel in Lake Pleasant, with almost sixty years of continuous operation by the same family. Beautifully located beside the outlet, it is a comfortable housing for guests, with modern appointments and excellent cuisine, yet with something of the nostalgic grandeur of an era gone by. The sweepingly exhilarating view from its porches of the full length of the lake is unsurpassed.

As leading residents of the area, the Osbornes have always been concerned with the promotion and welfare of the town. It was Bill Osborne who was instrumental in Lake Pleasant's reaching its apex in resort development through inducing world-championship prize fighters to use the Lower Adirondacks as their training grounds. Active in public affairs, Robert Osborne presently serves as county treasurer.

It was fortunate for Lake Pleasant that, when Will Osborne sought to settle in the mountains, he continued to the end of the road.

TOP OF THE COUNTY

THEY TELL at Long Lake that . . .

One clear winter day before the nineteenth century had moved into history, Mart Moody took down his muzzle-loading flintlock and set out on a hunting trip on the solid ice of Tupper Lake just over the Hamilton County line. His supply of meat was dangerously low. Worse still, he was virtually out of bullets, although his powder supply was adequate for current needs.

Suddenly, as he walked across the wind-swept ice, he spotted a furtive deer on the shore of the lake. Mart lay down in the snow and, sure enough, the unsuspecting deer started crossing the ice in his direction. Slowly, he took careful aim. As the deer sniffed and tarried, Mart happened to glance away from his gun-sights long enough to see a huge black bear crossing the frozen lake from the opposite shore.

This posed a serious problem. With only one last cartridge, Mart's single shot had to count. He decided to wait until the two forest animals crossed simultaneously past his poised gun. He had to get them both at the same time.

The strategy met with deserved success. Mart's single blast killed the deer all right and fortunately went straight through and killed the bear as well.

It represented a good day's work, and Mart Moody was mighty pleased as he dressed out the two animals he had bagged. He became curious as to what might have happened to that powerful bullet that seemed to have gone right through the bear's thick hide and out the other side.

To his gratification, he discovered that it had fiercely grazed a huge pine stump and that the splinters had killed both a partridge and a rabbit. Then it had seemed to have pierced a large tree. Searching for the bullet-hole in the tree, Mart's fingers came upon a sticky substance. He had shot into a bee's nest, he discovered. Soon he extracted a gelatine-like glob that represented a ten-quart pailful of honey.

Happily, the successful hunter started home, well-weighted with his newly-gained supplies. Mart was crossing a pine log over a stream when he slipped and fell into the brook. The icy waters were well over his waistline as he wallowed heavily to shore. Although the water seemed heavy where his trousers entered his boots, he was getting cold and figured he had better hurry home.

Reaching the inn which he ran at Moody, he deposited his game and removed his trousers. In them, he found twenty-five pounds of brook trout.

At least, that's the way Martin Moody told it, and he should have known.

Mart was a man for experiences like that. A son of Jacob Moody, the earliest settler at Saranac Lake, Mart was born in 1833. He came early to live on Tupper Lake and always ran a lodge for paying guests. He used to guide some of the most distinguished visitors to the Adirondacks, including Presidents Chester A. Arthur and Grover Cleveland. Mark Twain was sometimes a visitor at his inn. Yet probably nothing the noted author wrote could top the stories of his Adirondack host.

Moody and a companion were jacking deer one night, his friend paddling the boat while Moody handled the gun. Sure enough, their light shone right in the deer's eyes, temporarily blinding the animal. Mart got ready to fire. Suddenly, a huge black panther leaped on the deck of the boat.

"What did you do!" exclaimed a devoted listener, as Mart related the experience.

"I just brushed that panther aside and shot the deer," was Mart's ready reply.

Noted guests were not uncommon up at the top of Hamilton County at the turn of the century. And when young Annie Carey was being persuaded not to leave the companionship of friends at Long Lake Village to go to the Brandreth Tract, where her father was caretaker, it seemed reason enough and only small stretching of the truth to reply: "Father wants me up there to wait on table. The President's coming."

That evening, she was followed home by a group of neighbors that included Henry Kellogg and Walter Jennings, anxious to get a glimpse of their nation's chief executive. In disappointment, they returned to their homes.

As things turned out, Annie Carey's statement was not so untruthful, after all. Not long afterward, both President William Howard Taft and General John J. Pershing came to visit the proprietors of the Brandreth Tract.

Long Lake people remember the days when Ai Shaw (always with a capital "A," small "i," and pronounced "Aye-eye") used to run his sawmill. Having no lands of his own, Ai used to lick his lips greedily and yield to the overpowering temptation to cut logs on State land. He would be arrested and fined. He would have to go back and cut more timber off the same State-owned land in order to pay the tab.

Long Lakers like to repeat the unpredictable sayings of their good friend and neighbor, Alex Burnett. Alex is of French descent and has a way of mixing metaphors that would rival Samuel Goldwyn's well-earned fame.

He went over to Dr. Arpad G. Gerster's summer home one day to have a swelling removed from his head. The operation was most successful, and Alex was pleased. Asked if the doctor had given him an anesthetic, Alex shook his head.

"Naw," he replied. "He just poured on a little coca cola and cut it right off." Dr. Gerster would have called it Novocain.

One time, Alex Burnett was disgruntled with his family and was letting off steam to a friend.

"By jingo, if this keeps up," he promised, "I'm going to send my kids to perform school and put my wife in a house of corruption."

When the road was being paved to Blue Mountain Lake, Alex was one of the workers. A car drove up one day and the unsuspecting tourist asked the condition of the road to the south.

Alex looked at him in disdain.

"Don't you know that road's under instruction?" he taunted.

Adirondack tradition at Long Lake is being capably upheld.

TWENTY YEARS IN BED

THE NAMES of two old and well-known families of the Town of Hope were joined when, around 1870, John Bennett married Matilda Conklin's daughter, Sarah, and took her to live on his hillside farm along the old main road to Wells. Like most locations in the area, it was a beautifully scenic spot. The rear windows of the medium-sized house overlooked the valley flatlands. Beyond lay the wide rippling Sacandaga River with its multitudinous rocks worn smooth by centuries of spring freshets and heavy mid-summer rains. John Bennett's flatlands were as productive as any in the area.

A son named Fayette was born to the Bennetts in 1871 and five years later, a daughter, Maggie.

Sarah Bennett's children were her pride and joy. She raised them tenderly and with deep affection. It was her great delight when the family was blessed with three other children— George, born in 1879, Ward in 1882, and Frank in 1884.

As the only daughter, Maggie was her mother's particular delight. Maggie was never a sturdy child, and her growth was nursed in youngest years. Patience was rewarded as the frail young girl blossomed into mid-youthful years. Sarah devoted much of the attention she could afford from numerous, ever-present household chores to her little girl.

One day, the teen-age Maggie was struck with unaccountable illness. Sarah Bennett brought out all the home remedies that had been passed zealously from mother to daughter for generations past. Maggie's condition only worsened. The youthful chatter and carefree laughter gave way to the oppressive, ominous silence of the muted room. A distressed mother earnestly sought medical advice.

It was all to no avail. After a brief sickness, the beloved, youthful Maggie Bennett silently passed to another world.

A sorely distraught mother moved listlessly from the hushed and shadowed sick-room when it was over and done. Sarah Bennett grieved piteously. Hers was a bitter, hopeless mourning that knew no end.

As time passed, the woman began to undergo periods of undue stress. Her mind was found to wander. She would pursue routine activity with frenzied determination and furious rage. Such spells were followed by a return to normal living.

When, short years later, the epidemics of smallpox and black diphtheria moved into the mountains about the year 1893, Sarah Bennett showed sore distress. The stories that were brought to her door of deaths throughout the region brought deranged reaction. The memory of the deceased Maggie continued to hover with the mother. Never must such disaster be permitted to strike her family again.

Frantically, Sarah insisted that her husband harness the horses to the old wagon and take her with her three young sons to Northville for vaccinations. Her oldest son, Fayette, and Anna, his recent bride, then living with the family, were urged to take similar preventative measures. And when the family had returned from its journey, Sarah Bennett sent her boys scampering to the safety of their beds. Better that they should never leave the house at all than to suffer danger of contracting the malevolent, little-understood disease.

Fayette and Anna Bennett shortly went to live on a farm of their own. To them was born a daughter, whom they promptly named Maggie. Sarah Bennett was pleased.

There was little time to think of such things. The defense

of her three young sons weighed heavily on the woman's sturdy shoulders. At all costs, the boys must be kept in bed.

At first, their childish protests were often heard in the hillside farmhouse. But Sarah's metallic will was not to be outdone. They were sick, she told them, and must remain protected. As days became weeks and weeks became months, she convinced them that they were chronic invalids, destined for no other kind of life. Nor were the occasional remonstrances of the even-tempered John Bennett effective in gaining their release.

Years passed, and the family lived much to itself. The growing, bedded sons of John and Sarah Bennett, now crowding manhood, were never seen. Neighbors knew of their helplessness, but were powerless to intervene. Sarah's uneven temper and a loaded shotgun were her own defense.

The mother herself saw few people within the intervening decades. Sometimes, in the dark of an evening, while tortured by her mental wanderings, she would be seized with an uncontrollable desire to visit someone long-forgotten. Taking a kerosene lamp, she would walk up and down the dusty road that passed her unpainted, weatherbeaten house, searching for a person whose name and place of living she never knew.

At length, the sorely-troubled Sarah Bennett sought the solace of Sunday evening services at the mission church in Northville. It was apparent on her irregular visits to the house of worship that she was mentally unwell. "Bub" Snell, the welfare officer, together with Dr. J. Edward Grant, decided that, in all mercy, action must be taken. Nor would time wait.

The next Sunday evening, Sarah came as usual to the mission. As she left the little church, she was met by the two authorities, who tried to persuade the unreasoning woman to undergo medical care. When the panic-stricken Sarah started to bolt, strong hands held her firm. Wildly, she fought and thrashed to gain her freedom as she was being led unwillingly away. Sarah Bennett was placed in the State Asylum at Utica and given work in the laundry. There she remained until her death.

Released from the pathological tenderness of their maternal captor, the Bennett boys remained living the life they knew. Thoroughly convinced of their persistent ill-health, they continued to lie abed. It was only when a delegation from the Broadalbin Baptist Church came to the house on what they regarded as a mission of mercy that a change was made.

The State of New York is said to have taken charge. Treatment to develop flaccid, unused muscles was a primary requirement. Interrupted education was hastily begun.

In 1915, John Bennett, age seventy-one, and his three sons were living on the Bennett farm in the Town of Hope. The oldest son was thirty-five, the youngest, thirty. They were without occupation.

Ten years later, their father having gone to his reward, the three Bennett brothers were living together as bachelors on the family farm. George, the oldest, was the farmer. His brother, Ward, was a salesman. No occupation was given for Frank.

Ultimately, Ward became a barber and settled in Northville. Here he married and raised a family of two children. George became a caretaker. Frank suffered early death.

Sarah Bennett's solicitous care for her children was never fully overcome.

ADIRONDACK FUN

When Robb Stuart ran the corner store at Speculator, the boys would gather of an evening around the old pot-bellied stove to swap stories. It gave Robb something of the feeling of presiding at executive sessions as village leader. That was why Robb always insisted on seeing justice done. Robb was a well-liked, amiable fellow, who could sometimes become cranky as well.

It was during the Great Depression, when money was scarce, work was scant, and people were doing everything possible to earn even small amounts of badly needed cash. Robb Stuart was travelling down the back road to Wells. Suddenly, his eyes hit upon a stripped piece of forest land where some-one had been cutting Christmas trees. What is more, it was right squarely on State-owned land.

Robb's indignation rose. The more he thought about it, the angrier he became.

At the first opportunity, the store-keeper went straight to Sheriff George Perkins and Ranger Roberts. Something had to be done, he proclaimed. With a formal complaint of this kind, action was, indeed, required.

Sheriff and ranger drove down the bumpy road toward Wells and secreted themselves and their automobile in the nearby underbrush. When at length the man came to gather his trees, they nabbed him dead to rights.

To Robb Stuart's chagrin, the culprit turned out to be his own brother. Since he had no spare money, Robb himself was required to pay the fine.

* * * * *

When the American Legion Post held its annual dinner at Osborne's Inn in Speculator, Pants Lawrence, the inveterate raconteur, was an invited guest. Knowing they were in for

Hunters' Cabin at T Lake used by Henry Courtney, John Burtin, and George and Hobe Casler.

Osborne Inn, Speculator, built in 1902, served as a landmark for over sixty years.

View of Long Lake, showing the famous Sagamore Hotel, razed in 1960.

a treat, the members could scarcely wait to dispense with normal business before calling on the old guide for an auto-biographical tale.

"Maybe you haven't heard about the time that me and my brother, Abe, went out hunting deer," remarked Pants casually, as he came to his feet. "Now both Abe and me thought we were the better hunter. So we agreed that whichever got the first deer, it was his.

"Well, it wasn't long before we both spied a big ten-point buck pushing its nose out of the brush. We both raised our rifles at the same time and the guns fired at once. The deer keeled over dead. When we went to look it over, there was only one bullet hole in its body.

"Each of us claimed we'd shot that buck and, before long, the argument got plenty hot. There was just one way to settle it. We decided to have a duel and shoot it out.

"Well, we backed away from each other, levelled our rifles and both fired at the same time. Nothing happened at all. So we decided to call the whole thing off and go home. But we just couldn't figure it out.

"That evening, Abe called me on the telephone. 'Have you cleaned your gun yet, Pants?' he asked.

" 'No, I haven't,' I said.

" 'Well, when you do, you'll find my bullet backwards in your own gun barrel,' Abe told me. 'Yours was in mine.' "

* * * * *

Hughey Mitchell had returned from the Civil War and had opened a saloon in the southern part of Wellstown near Jim and Pat Mitchell's hotel. It was pleasant to renew acquaintances in the area, he found. The place had changed quite a bit since he had shouldered his gun.

One day, he chanced to meet an approachable young fellow whose conversation he thoroughly enjoyed. Unknown to Hughey, it was the new domine from the neighboring Town of Hope.

After visiting for a time and swapping stories, Hughey became interested in his new-found companion.

"What's your occupation?" he asked with a smile.

"I'm a minister," explained the other. "I preach the Gospel." As Hughey gulped unbelievingly, the stranger added: "What's your vocation?"

Hughey did some quick thinking. "Mine is much the same as yours," the saloon-keeper from the mountain village answered. "We're both about the same distance from our base of supplies."

* * * * *

When John Thompson harnessed his yoke of white oxen to his two-wheeled cart and made his weekly journey down the West River road to Wells for supplies, it was fairly certain that the barrooms of the local hotels were to do a substantial business.

After one such visit, John weaved uncertainly out to his conveyance and started down the road. Driving slowly up the West Hill road, he found his eyelids drooping heavily and his body becoming tired. John lay down in the back of the wagon for some needed sleep.

An hour or two later, a passing neighbor quietly surveyed the situation and decided to unyoke the oxen and let them find their quiet way home.

When the sleeping farmer finally came to life, he rubbed sleep from his eyes, gingerly touched his throbbing temples, and came to a sitting position in his cart.

"Am I John Thompson or am I not John Thompson?" he queried. "If I am John Thompson, I've lost a yoke of oxen. If I'm not John Thompson, I've found a cart."

* * * * *

Herb Hall of Speculator used to head off into the woods hunting and, before he was seen again, a full year had often passed. Herb would come pounding down from the mountains, repair shortly to a local barroom, and would assuredly make up for lost time.

Dropping his gear in preparation for his first evening's contact with civilization, Herb could be heard muttering to himself.

"I've got to go out and get drunk tonight, and how I dread it," the old huntsman would lament.

* * * * *

A male resident of the Southern Adirondacks was experiencing his first visit to New York City with cautious enjoyment. All of the sights must be seen.

There were the tall buildings, the automat, a motion picture theatre, and a major league baseball game. By no means to be overlooked was travel on the subway.

The short-statured, muscular lumberjack reached the subsurface transit lines at rush hour. The surging mass of humanity fairly swept him onto the crowded train.

Standing among the hard-packed populace, the lumberjack found the ample foot of an oversized gentleman planted firmly on his own. Patience gave way to irritation, as the discomfort persisted. Defiantly, the mountain man looked up into the other's face.

"By jees, I wish I had a peavey hook," he muttered darkly, "and I'd get your big foot off from mine."

The considerable New Yorker's response was a surprised expression. They say he still wonders at times about the fate with which he was threatened.

THE PRIZE-FIGHTERS' TRAINING
GROUNDS

THE ADVENT of World War I found the men of the Adirondacks ready to rally to their country's cause.

Bill Osborne was one of the first to go, enlisting in the U.S.
Marine Corps at the Philadelphia military base on May 28,
1917. Bill saw service with the American Expeditionary Forces
in France and was twice-wounded in action.

While overseas, Bill found in his outfit a pale, diffident, little-
understood tent-mate, who liked to box. And box he did, going
all-out for the amateur prize-fights staged for the entertainment
of the men. All in all, he was an unusual person—clean-cut,
high-minded, yet always a winner, fair and square. His name
was Gene Tunney. He and Bill Osborne became pals, and Bill
held his bathrobe and towel while Gene fought in the soldier
shows.

During the war, Tunney confided to some of his intimates
in the marine unit that he would like to make prize-fighting his
career. He insisted he could beat the world heavyweight champion without trouble. Tunney was much more certain of winning than were his associates. Nevertheless, Bill gave him
encouragement and an idea as well.

"Gene," he said, "if you really want a winning place to
train, I can tell you where. You just come up to my place at
Lake Pleasant. Roam those mountains, live in that invigorating
air, and eat my mother's cooking. You can't lose."

Gene promised that, if he ever reached the top of the
heavyweight class, he would do just that. They separated, Osborne returning in February, 1919, with the casual company
that served as guard for President Wilson. He was discharged
in May, 1919, at Quantico.

Seven years later, Gene Tunney, the professional prize-fighter, had reason to remember Bill Osborne's words. He was signed for the toughest fight of his career, the world heavyweight championship bout against the invincible Jack Dempsey. He needed all the support he could get. Bill Osborne's suggestion rang in his ears.

"We'll train at Lake Pleasant," he told his associates. Bill Osborne was amazed to get a wire saying: "Make room for me. Here I come to make good my promise given to you in France."

Tunney came to the Osborne Inn at Speculator and stayed to train for each of his three championship fights from 1926 through 1928. He was delighted with his and Osborne's choice. Speculator became his legal residence. Gene did his voting there. Thanks to his influence and prestige, Speculator became a famous resort. For this was the period when society had selected prize-fighting as its foremost fad.

"Those were great days in the fight racket, those days with Tunney at Speculator," wrote Bill Corum in his syndicated column. "Pugilism had just been taken up in a glittering way by what Tex Rickard delighted to describe as 'the best people,' and there were times when millionaires were so thick underfoot that you had to fight your way through them to buy a picture post card at the drug store.

"It was nothing in those days to see the president of twenty-six ten-million-dollar corporations and a member of the board of directors of forty-six more galloping across the big road with a bucket and sponge to minister to the needs of some ex-truck driver in a pair of unwashed woolen drawers, who had nicknamed himself a prize-fighter.

"You would be waiting around the lobby of Will Osborne's tavern to use the only telephone and you could not help but hear the gentleman in the turtle-neck sweater in the booth bellowing: 'Tell Magruder to buy me three thousand stell at the opening.' And the gentleman wouldn't have the receiver hook down either. That is, in most cases, he wouldn't.

"They came, those well-known men, with their friends and

lady friends to the daily workouts in sleek black limousines, on special trains and by flying machines. There was that late afternoon when Bernard Gimbel, one of the few who really knew what it was all about, and my friend Sam Pryor, and Charles V. Bobb (and whatever became of good-time Charley anyhow?) trying to take off from the ninth green of the golf course and didn't, and missed death by the faintest of whispers . . .

"No doubt the affluence and importance of the customers added something to the glamour that seemed to surround the fighters and the game itself. I don't know. I only know that there are no training camps like that these days . . ."

This was the time that a group of forty men came from New York by special train to see Tunney spar. "Wealth of America in Speculator," a newspaper headline read. Bernard Gimbel was a close friend. Philadelphia's J. Drexel Biddle came, and when Osborne provided a tent for the financier, another for his wife, and a third for his chauffeur until accommodations could be found in the crowded Osborne Inns, Biddle was most grateful. And there were hosts of others of equal note on hand.

Tunney was as well-liked by the mountain residents as he seemed to like them. He would walk up the street where young Gerald Buyce and his chums would be playing under the lilac bushes in the family's front yard. He would return from the village with a bag of candy for the kids. Young Bill Osborne was his constant companion.

One day, while he was out for road work, Tunney found a crew putting up poles for the village lighting. He stopped at once, grabbed a pike pole and started to work. Lew Fink, his trainer, came along about that time and scolded him soundly.

Pants Lawrence was a loyal companion who used to take Tunney on daily hikes in the woodlands. "Neighbors like Pants make my training camp in Speculator a delightful place in which to train for a fight," the boxer asserted. "All the natural advantages that contribute to build up one's body and mind are present and the interest of the townsfolk, instead of being an annoyance as is often found in cities, is an added impetus to development. Local pride in the mountain resort is contagious . . ."

But Tunney drew the line on a statement made by a native whom he encountered during his road work.

"Mr. Tunney," the man told him, "I can tell you truthfully that any fighter who trains up in these mountains which God made Himself, can never be licked by any man."

The training ring was set up back of the taproom. Tunney was housed with reporters in the building that now serves as taproom. He was moved to a private cottage down the road when the place became noisy. He and Bill Osborne usually had their meals served in Bill's private office at the lower inn.

Tunney proved a very sociable person but shied from publicity. He always liked to meet people who wanted to meet Gene Tunney. He was reluctant to meet those who wanted to meet the champion of the world.

The first Dempsey fight was set for September 23, 1926 at Philadelphia. A technicality required that Tunney be a resident of the State for twenty-one days preceding the match. He accomplished final training at Stroudsburg.

When the prize-fighter was about to fly off to the bout, the lake was mirror-calm and the plane could not make its take-off until motor boats roughed up the lake's surface. The kids of the area stood watching with tears streaming down their small ruddy cheeks: Gene Tunney was going away.

Tunney was completely confident of his ability to defeat the Manassa Mauler. Bill and Robert Osborne and Ray Campbell of the Cleveland News, took him to Stroudsburg. En route, Tunney handed Bill a blank check. It was backed by all kinds of funds, Gene told Osborne. "Don't be afraid to bet anything you want on the fight," he said.

Tunney fully lived up to his own forecast at the greatest of fights. A new world's champion was born in the ring that night as Dempsey went down to defeat after ten rounds. Bill Osborne's wartime promise had rung as true as the final gong.

Yet the whole thing seemed incredible to the fighting world. Surely, it was a fluke. It could not possibly happen twice. Jack Dempsey rechallenged. Tunney returned to Speculator to train.

Prior to his return bout with Dempsey, scheduled for September 22, 1927 at Chicago's Soldier's Field, the champion was again required to spend twenty-one days in the host State. The fight itself proved a glamorous occasion. "Society turned out en masse," the newspapers emoted, "most of the women wearing orchids." The ample audience sparkled with celebrities.

"There was the delicately golden Mrs. Philip D. Armour in pale beige of sports clothes persuasion," wrote the enraptured society editor of the *Chicago Evening American*. "Notwithstanding this, she wore a triple strand of pearls. Mrs. Leander McCormick was also in a daytime costume . . . and Alice Cudahy. Mrs. Knowlton L. Ames, Jr. wore an orchid boutonniere on a very smart though simple suit of dark color, and a trig little hat set her off very smartly. Mrs. Roy Howard and Mrs. Bernard Gimbel . . . rather put the Chicago women in the shade . . ."

The star-studded names seemed endless. It was the biggest gate in ring history. Over a million dollars came to Gene.

The wonder was that, with such an audience, anyone bothered to watch the fight at all. Yet it proved an historic battle, one that is still argued in fighting circles. Dempsey knocked Tunney to the mat, then, contrary to Chicago rules, moved to his own corner. Referee Dave Barry, after motioning and partly conducting Dempsey to the neutral corner, returned and picked up the count, thereby giving Tunney an extra four seconds. Tunney rose dazedly to his feet at the count of "ten," staring at Dempsey as though he were an apparition. The bell ended the round.

There were those who insisted that, without the extra four seconds, Tunney would have been unable to regain his feet. Others maintain as vehemently that he was merely wisely using his full respite. Insiders say that the disputed point became a build-up for a third fight that never came off.

In any case, two records were broken when Gene went down in the seventh round. It was the first time that any man whom Jack Dempsey ever sent crashing to the canvas got up to stay, and it was the first time that Gene Tunney was ever off his feet. The decision went to Tunney.

Gene returned to Speculator to train for his bout with Tom Heeney at New York's Yankee Stadium. Afterwards, Bill Corum wrote that when the champion left for the bout, he was "the best trained and best equipped fighting man I have ever seen. He had reached that peak that comes once, and only once, to any man in any profession."

The contender was knocked out in the eleventh round. Soon afterward, Tunney announced his retirement from the ring and married the former Polly Lauder.

Although he removed his residency from Speculator, it was a place he never forgot. Correspondence continues with his marine buddy, Bill Osborne. Gene talks of his former neighbors in the Adirondacks and praises Bill's mother's pies. "I've never tasted anything like them since," he affirms.

The people of Lake Pleasant have a nostalgic feeling for Gene Tunney, too. The place has never been quite the same.

BILL OSBORNE'S PANTS

TALL, GOOD-NATURED Frank "Pants" Lawrence could be found almost anywhere in the Lake Pleasant area where people gathered and friendly conversation ensued. One of the favorite hang-outs of the veteran guide was the Osborne Inn when it became the focal center for a large segment of the sporting world. Here Pants met, enjoyed, and overjoyed the country's boxing elite and their large social following of the day. And when it came time for the world championship prize-fighters to leave their training camp at Osborne's Inn in final preparation for their major bouts, Pants somehow always got invited along.

As Gene Tunney's return match with Jack Dempsey approached, the name of Pants Lawrence was widely mentioned. Clara Osborne uttered a sigh. "Does Pants have to be with us *everywhere* we go?" she murmured.

Two days before Bill and Clara Osborne were to entrain for Chicago, a disconsolate Pants entered the hotel.

"I guess I won't be going to the fight," he announced sadly. "I've got stomach poisoning from some stale bread I ate."

The situation was apparent at a glance. Pants never had money of his own for journeys of that kind. Somehow in the haste of last-minute preparations, no invitation had been extended the old guide to travel as one of the party's guests.

Bill cast a meaningful side-look at Mrs. Osborne. "I guess we'll have to change our reservations to Chicago," he said. Clara nodded her assent.

Asked to accompany the hotel owner and his wife, Pants found his health instantly improved. He was right along with the Osbornes, and at their expense, as the train flew westward toward the Windy City.

World Champion Gene Tunney used to roar with laughter at Pants' stories of his travels to Chicago. The prize-fighter particularly enjoyed the sequence about the mountain man's initial experience in a sleeping car.

"I looked behind them curtains and stretched myself out for a rehearsal," Pants would relate. "When I found myself travelling feet first, I got up. 'There's only one person that goes that way,' I says to myself, 'and Pants Lawrence ain't that kind yet.'

"There was a friendly sort of conductor on the car and him and me spent the rest of the night chattin' in the smokin' part.

"When we neared Chicago the next mornin', I reckoned as how Bill Osborne might be sore if he seen I hadn't been to bed all night so I went back to find that turned-wrong bed.

"Well, I'd forgot to take down the number and in the dark they all looked alike. First, I reckoned as how I'd try the end one, but when a big foot came out to hit me in the face, I knew that wusn't mine. The one that next looked like mine returned a little scream of a woman's voice when I pushed back the curtain.

"I wuz ready to call it a day then, but the colored fellow heard the commotion and steered me into the empty one. I took a stretch for a couple of minutes to rumple it up some, then when daylight came along, I hopped out.

"If I don't see this next Heeney scrap, Gene, there'll be one disappointed fella here in Speculator, but if I have to ride one of them fortune-tellin' sleepin' booths, I guess I'm out."

When Pants was elected sheriff of Hamilton County, former Governor Alfred E. Smith was serving as sheriff in New York City while marking time for his next successful gubernatorial campaign. As a prize-fighting enthusiast, Al was often seen at Osborne's Inn. There he met Pants Lawrence, of course, as everyone sooner or later did. On one of his visits, the New York State governor brought Pants a custom-made badge for the sheriff of Hamilton County. At the top, in small letters, the name "Pants" was engraved.

Pants treasured the star, wore it regularly, displayed it often.

He found, when he attended Gene Tunney's championship matches, the insignia gave him standing.

As his final illness struck and he was kept confined to his home, the old guide was unhappy over his inability to see and talk with his numerous friends. It wasn't right for a man like Pants. The pronouncement that he would have to be removed to a nursing home in Gloversville proved the climax of his gloom.

Leaving his house with effort one day, the veteran woodsman made his way sadly to the Osborne Inn, scene of the most pleasant of his life's experiences. Reaching Bill Osborne's front desk, he slumped heavily into a chair. Wordlessly, he extended his gnarled, weatherbeaten hand. Bill saw the cherished sheriff's badge in the gaunt man's bony palm.

"I want you to have this," Pants told the hotel proprietor.

Inwardly moved but stern-faced throughout, Bill knew it was the time to talk gruffly.

"I don't want it," he replied.

"Yes, Bill, it's for you," Pants insisted. "You and Al and I have always been friends."

Once more, Bill demurred.

"All right, then keep it in your safe," directed Pants, with something of his old vigor, "and give it to the first goddamn Democrat sheriff that gets elected."

In deference to the old guide's wishes, Bill placed the badge carefully in his hotel safe. There it remains. There hasn't been another Democrat sheriff in Hamilton County for the past thirty years.

THE TALES THEY TOLD

THERE WERE strange happenings in the Adirondacks around the turn of the century. Surprising as they seemed, the truth of each was not to be doubted. They were told by the people who had experienced them, proof enough of their authenticity.

There was, for example, the experience of Mart Moody up Tupper Lake way. Moody was hunting one cold winter's day when he came out of the woods on the bank of a lake. On the far side was a campfire and, despite the distance, Moody decided to approach it and get warm. As he neared the fire, he could feel no heat. It was only when he had doffed one mitten that he realized the blaze before him was frozen completely static in the cold, cold air.

Sheriff Frank "Pants" Lawrence was a man for unusual experiences. Nor did he ever seem to keep them to himself.

When smokeless powder was coming into use, the sportsmen were bringing it into the mountains instead of the more orthodox black. "Pants" was skeptical. It was the old black powder that packed the real charge, he knew.

Nevertheless, he was willing to give the new powder an honest try. Pants was an expert marksman, so good in fact that he never had to bother with traps. He could just take a rifle and shoot a muskrat in the eye. This time, he was trying the new smokeless powder.

As he walked up the stream, he spotted a muskrat, drew careful bead and fired. Then he walked over to pick up the animal, only to find that it had slipped safely into the water, causing him the loss of a skin worth from thirty-five to forty cents. Shaking his head, he paused to reload his rifle. No sooner had he rammed the ball home than he saw another "rat." Again, he took careful aim and fired, then ran quickly to the spot. But the muskrat, unharmed, had scurried away.

[189]

Pants was getting mighty disturbed. This time, he took a double load of powder and took special care in the reloading. He took off his mackinaw, pushed back his cap, and made ready to run for the next muskrat he shot.

As he fired, he was away like a shot, hardly knowing whether the gun had cracked or not. Running up the bank to the exact spot where the muskrat should have been, he leaned over to pull it out of the water, when along came the ball out of his own musket and hit him squarely in the seat of the pants.

It was proof enough for anyone. Pants never used smokeless powder thereafter.

Then there was Old Charlie Letson, who took his dog out one day and ran it until he got into Canada. Asked how he got across the St. Lawrence River, Letson thought a minute.

"Guess I just went around it," he replied.

One day, Pants Lawrence started out from camp, thinking he might find a bear. Not expecting to travel far or for long, he did not take much ammunition. But it was one of those days that make a fellow want to see what's behind the next tree and over the next rise of ground.

Before he knew it, Pants had ranged many miles and the day was drawing to a close. He had little to show for his expedition. He had seen no bear. He had shot at some small game and had had a go at a couple of deer. As a result, he had little powder and no lead at all as he walked homeward down the mountain trail.

Suddenly, he was aware of a stealthy movement beside the trail to his right. As he paused, he saw a panther's tail whipping to and fro above the grass nearby. Pants knew from the movement of that tail that here was a panther ready to spring. And he was powerless to fire his empty gun!

Pants ducked as the black animal sprang through the air. The panther sailed right over his head.

Instantly, the angry beast whirled and sprang once more. Just in time, Pants dropped to his knee. Once more the panther landed on the far side of the mountain path.

This time, Pants knew the animal would turn more rapidly. Sure enough, as he glanced out of the corner of his eye, he could see it, tail lashing in fury, ready for another leap.

Crouched on all fours and fumbling for his knife, Pants dropped flat to the ground. He could almost feel the cat's claws as it passed over his head. Quickly, he rolled on his back, knife upraised, and waited for what might well be the panther's last jump.

Nothing happened. After an interval, Pants rose slowly to his feet. To his amazement, the panther was stalking slowly away beyond the grass and up the mountainside.

Pants decided to follow. What, he wondered, would make a hungry beast, angry enough to pounce three times, so quickly give up his quest? He followed it for more than a mile.

Finally, up where the timber began to thin and a relatively flat grassy area came into view, Pants parted the "popple" branches and peered through. There on the out-cropping of rock, Pants watched transfixed. The panther was practising shorter jumps.

"Kib" Ostrander, who ran a store for several years in Speculator, was credited with the account of a big muscallonge caught by "Barb" Satterlee over in the Lewey Lake section.

"It was brought down here to the store and placed on exhibition," Kib told. "It was some big fish."

After the fish had remained with him for a while, Kib noticed a lump on its stomach. Promptly, he cut it open. There was a mighty rush and flapping of wings and away flew a big wild duck. And when he looked inside the fish, there was a nest with four eggs on which the duck had been sitting.

The listener to this tale stared in dumb wonderment at the apparent size of the fish. As a shadow of doubt crossed the man's face, Kib clinched the story.

The duck flew over by Pants Lawrence's hotel and was shot and served for dinner to appease the voracious appetites of Tom Kelly and "Doc" McMonagle, two of his guests, Kib related. Both men would vouch for the truthfulness of the incident.

And there was Elmer Houghtaling of Gloversville who used to be the taxidermist for the people of the Southern Adirondacks. Elmer had his own unique way of getting rabbits.

He would go out on a cold night in winter and build a fire in a swamp, letting the coals burn to embers. The rabbits would come and sit around the comfortable low fire to get warm. Unknown to themselves, they would freeze right there. Elmer would merely have to go around and knock them in the head. He said he could get any number of cottontails in this way.

Strange goings-on for any community. But in the Adirondacks, such unusual happenings never ceased.

HOW TO GET A WIFE

IN THE DARK DAYS of the depression in the 1930's, when people were signed for government-instituted work at the local level, an interviewer for the WPA encountered at Lake Pleasant a situation for which he was ill-prepared.

The usual routine questions were being asked of a resident of the area.

"Are you married?"

"Yes."

"Have any children?"

"Yes."

"Number of dependents?"

"None."

The interviewer relaxed his grip on his pencil and looked up sharply. "What about your wife?"

"Sold her."

The interrogator grasped the sides of the table at which he wrote. "You what!"

"Sure. I sold her. If you don't believe me, I'll show you the bill of sale."

Unnerved but undefeated, the government interviewer continued with his work. He had inadvertently run head-on into a story, locally known but seldom told.

The man was the product of a remote part of the community, separated from the main thoroughfares by a hindering ridge of hills. Its lands had never been as rich and rolling as those along Lake Pleasant's shores. Many of the earliest settlers there made only token clearing of the land. Instead, they worked in the few small occupations open to them—shingle-making, spruce-gum picking, lumbering, or trapping. Down through the years, it became a poorer part of the community. As time went on, it became separated by manners and mores as well.

There was amusement, if not surprise, the day one of this community's male residents strode eagerly into Edgar Call's general store at Lake Pleasant Village. He was a diminutive person in his early thirties, but he bore a full-sized request.

It seemed he required a bill-of-sale executed, with witnesses thereto. He wanted to sell his wife to a neighbor in exchange, some say, for ten dollars and a pig. And he wanted to make sure that the purchaser did not merely keep the woman during the summer while living was inexpensive, only to return her when the more costly winter season set in. This was to be a sale that must stick.

As a member of a long line of grocers for some generations, Ed Call was accustomed to unusual requests. But this one had him stumped.

"I guess we'd better go across to the county buildings," he said. Here at least, a typewriter could be found, if not official sanction, the storekeeper felt.

Thanks to highly amused but equally considerate neighbors, the satisfied petitioner left with the bill-of-sale tucked safely in his pocket. The transaction was duly made and the newly-joined couple lived together—happily, it is assumed—until their deaths a few years ago.

Immediately, this community apart from the community assumed new interest as the incident was described. Other strange stories issued from the area, many of them no doubt untrue. Occasionally, the section earned unmerited reputation.

In the early days of the State campsite at Moffitt's Beach, a camper agreed one evening to take a neighboring camper's dog for a stroll. At length, man and dog found themselves on a road apart from the main highways.

As they approached a small house, the dog set out in pursuit of one of the hens wandering in the dooryard. The fowl was straightway captured and killed.

An enraged housewife appeared on the porch and loudly demanded payment for her loss. Harsh words were exchanged as the man refused to part with money in behalf of a dog that was not his own and over which he had no control.

At that moment, a young mountain man appeared quietly in the doorway.

"Git the gun, maw," he drawled, "an' I'll shoot 'im."

The city visitor blanched and fell back. Turning, he began hastily retracing his footsteps down the road. The farther he went, the faster he strode. By the time he had reached the campsite entrance, he was virtually in a dead run.

Breathlessly, he recounted his experience to the ranger.

"Do you think he really would have shot me?" he gasped. And before the ranger could reply, the man had fled to the safety and anonymity of numbers toward the lake shore.

Undoubtedly, he has retold often about the time he was almost murdered in cold blood at Lake Pleasant, oblivious to the fact that the mountain resident had threatened the dog, not the man.

THE DISAPPEARANCE OF
CARLETON BANKER

THE DREAD ALARM of "lost man" was sounded throughout the Southern Adirondacks on Saturday, November 11, 1916, and half a hundred men dropped routine tasks for urgent, agonizing search. Systematic combing of every trail and bypath was begun in the dense woods back of Piseco Lake and into the Jessup River country beyond.

The object was Carleton Banker of Gloversville.

The previous Wednesday, a party of seven executives and employees of the F. J. & G. Railroad had left Gloversville for their annual hunting expedition in the Piseco region. The camp of Truman Lawrence became their headquarters, as in previous years.

After an unsuccessful Thursday on the runways, Carleton Banker, superintendent of the Cayadutta division of the upstate railroad, and Frederick A. Bagg, the railroad's engineer, walked to the remote mountain cabin of the hermit, "Foxey" Brown.

The very location held ominous sound for numerous residents and visitors to the area. Foxey Brown was the region's most legendary hermit. His was a suspicious past and an awesome present. He had lived there, a recluse, for some twenty-five years.

Foxey's real name was David Brennan, a railroad man, who had come to the wilderness to escape the forces of the law. He was said to have pounded up a man in his native Boston and had left thinking his victim dead.

For a time, he worked in the lumber woods around Lake Pleasant. Then, struck by a falling tree, he became unsuited for the strenuous work and settled in the woodlands about six miles back of Piseco. There on Fall Stream, he built a comfortable little camp with a barn, and raised cattle, cutting grass on the vlaie for hay. Occasionally, he would supplement his meager income by making shingles, which he exchanged for food.

The bearded Foxey was described as a gruff old fellow, whose bark was worse than his bite. No one was permitted near his camp.

"Get out of here or I'll send lead for sinkers!" he would shout at a trespasser. And he was not joking. On three different occasions, he shot at Charlie Preston, the game warden, who later became his friend. On the rare occasions when he came to the village for supplies, he would stalk firmly up and down the road. The terrified housewives would hastily withdraw and lock their doors.

As the years passed, old Foxey mellowed somewhat and gained a limited number of friends. One was Carleton Banker, who started a bank account for the hermit and brought him clothing in the fall of the year. It was this friendship that brought Bagg and Banker to Foxey's camp that bleak November day.

The trio hunted on Friday, and Banker shot a small deer. Because he complained of an aching leg, he was stationed that afternoon at the end of a deer run while Bagg hunted with the hermit. As daylight waned, Foxey Brown left to find Banker.

It was after 5 o'clock and darkness had fallen when next Bagg met Foxey. The hermit was alone. Banker was not at the appointed place, he said. Bagg fired a signal shot and got one faintly in reply from the direction where Banker had been left.

Hermit and hunter returned to camp to await Carleton Banker. They prepared supper and, when Banker failed to arrive, ate their food and rested briefly. No real concern was felt since Banker was experienced in woodsmanship and knew the area well. By 7 o'clock, fears were rising. For five hours, the two men searched the darkly-shadowed woodland depths with lantern. There were no answers to their signal shots and at 11 o'clock the search was abandoned. Carleton Banker could amply fend for himself for a night in the woods.

Early Saturday morning, the search was renewed over a wider area. Footprints were found, but they appeared too large for Banker's notably small shoes. At one o'clock Saturday afternoon, Bagg started frantically to Piseco for help. Two separate parties were hastily organized to search throughout the night and the following day.

By early Sunday morning, fully fifty men were scouring the timberlands over a fifty-mile area. As darkness fell that evening, the hunter remained missing in the blackness and clues were painfully slight. One man told of finding footprints made by a small shoe, only to lose the trail. Someone had located an abandoned temporary camp. Another report told that a dead deer, with part of the venison missing, had been discovered.

Mrs. Banker and her two daughters were notified in Gloversville.

By Monday afternoon, tension was at its height. Additional searching parties were at work. Footsteps made by a small shoe were found in the Mossy Vlaie section. The man had taken short steps and had sat down frequently to rest, obviously near exhaustion. Guides followed the trail until darkness, when the search was necessarily abandoned until the following day. It seemed obvious that Banker did not know in which direction he was travelling. He might be found at any point. Clouds had hidden the sun since Saturday, removing one sign the lost hunter might have used to find his way.

The weather remained damp and cold. On Monday night, six inches of dreaded snow drifted treacherously down.

Nevertheless, hope persisted, as fully a hundred men entered the woods on Tuesday morning for a last determined drive. Bloodhounds from Rome, N.Y. arrived in Gloversville in a blinding snowstorm at 10 o'clock that morning and were taken immediately to the north country.

By Wednesday afternoon, all hope was virtually abandoned of finding Carleton Banker alive. Every clue had been run to earth and every report had proved mere myth. Some of the searching parties were returning from the 120-hour-long quest.

Although the weather had warmed, more snow had fallen. Fully eight inches now covered the rough mountainous terrain. The bloodhounds that had been placed on Fall Stream trail had proved ineffectual. The Mossy Vlaie country had been covered closely and the hope that had risen the previous morning when signal shots were heard, had been dispelled. The feeling grew that the lost man was not far from where he had been last seen, that he had possibly been shot by another hunter or had died from a sudden heart attack.

Clairvoyants were consulted. They told that Banker would be found near the place where Bagg and Brown had left him, lying face down.

The futile, hopeless search was reluctantly discontinued on Thursday. Conviction grew that the body might never be found and that the manner of death would go down "as another of the unsolved mysteries of Hamilton County."

As time elapsed and rumors and conjecture persisted, the finger of suspicion was pointed increasingly at the old hermit, Foxey Brown. Sadly, the aged mountain man turned one day to Charlie Preston.

"You don't think I killed Banker, do you, Charlie?" he beseeched. "No one should. He's always done things for me, always took care of my money."

Charlie expressed confidence in the hermit's innocence.

"I'm going away," Foxey said. "I got a gun of Cy Dunham's that you can have."

Before his departure from the mountains, Foxey learned that he had never been held guilty of crime in Boston. Delivering his blankets to Bill Gallagher, he set out. Some time later, Gallagher received a letter from Foxey from a mid-southern state, asking that his blankets be sent.

Six years passed. On Friday, November 10, 1922—just six years to the day from the time when Carleton Banker was lost—Bill Abrams, the guide, went into the forest north of

Piseco Lake. He had reached a point a short distance from the Spruce Lake trail, when he was attracted by the glint of a tin tobacco can glistening in the sun.

Abrams kicked meditatively at the can, dislodging an accumulation of twigs. Beneath lay a bone. Again, he kicked at the leaves. Additional bones were uncovered. They were those of a human body. Abrams returned at once to Piseco and notified the county coroner at Wells.

The pliable bones, softened through the evaporation of their lime content, represented only a small part of the body. But the possessions laying near at hand were unmistakable. Identification of the objects was made at Wells by the Misses Helen and Marian Banker and Attorney William Baker.

Carleton Banker's body had been discovered almost within call of Piseco. He had died three miles from Piseco Village and five miles from the spot where he had been left by his friends.

THE HUNTER HATES THE HUNT

OF ALL the occupations he ever undertook—and like most mountain men, he engaged in a variety of pursuits—none appealed more to Sandford Courtney than that of guide. Born to the mountains, he liked to hike the wooded trails with a gun. Scaring up an errant deer was a distinct thrill and bagging a buck was his greatest joy.

The second time he ever shot a rifle, San killed a bear. He was fifteen at the time and the year was 1897. After that, he was never more content than when hunting through the thick green forests that stretch for miles around his Lake Pleasant home.

San Courtney was an accomplished woodsman and guide.

Following in the footsteps of his father, Warren Courtney, he proudly led parties from all over the State.

One day, it suddenly ended. In one short, horror-filled instant, the joy of hunting had miserably paled, the lure of the woodlands was irrevocably gone.

The hunting party that was planned for Sunday, November 10, 1940 was anticipated with a great deal of relish. Levi Worden and his son-in-law and daughter, Bill and Madeline Richer, were coming up from Fayetteville near Syracuse. Sandford Courtney had guided them many times.

Sandford liked to stop in at the home of his son-in-law and daughter, Bill and Caroline Rose Lamphier, to see his two young grandchildren. He combined his current visit with an invitation to Bill to join the party in the forthcoming hunt. He figured they would head out over Fish Mountain, San said, an area that should easily hold promise of game. Bill agreed that it sounded like good sport.

The down-state sportsmen arrived on the appointed day and the group moved off into the woods. About seven miles from Lake Pleasant, they set up stations. San Courtney and Bill Richer were to do the driving, while Bill Lamphier and Fayetteville's police chief, Levi Worden, were placed on watches.

It was early afternoon when the large buck was encountered. Pursuing it stealthily, the two stalkers reached a small swamp and Courtney offered to exchange positions. Richer was not used to the woods.

At the far end of the runway, Bill Lamphier, clad in khaki flannel shirt and khaki trousers, heard the frightened buck crashing through the underbrush. It seemed to be moving off to the left rather than directly toward him. He was determined that the truant, fleet-footed animal must not escape. Leaving his watch, he moved silently behind a wall of shrubs toward Levi Worden's station.

Suddenly, Worden became alert. He, too, heard the fleeing buck. There was movement in the brush before him. There was color—the color of a deer's soft furry coat. Steadily, he raised the 35-calibre pump gun he carried. Taking careful aim, he fired.

By now, the drivers had neared the spot. Courtney heard the shot and hastened toward Worden. As he strode through the surrounding screen of trees, he saw Richer standing white-faced and trembling.

"Worden killed Bill!" he screamed in terror.

Uncomprehendingly, Courtney ran toward Worden, who was rolling and tumbling on the ground.

"No, Bill is shot!" Richer called hoarsely after him.

Sandford Courtney located his son-in-law's body. Bill Lamphier had been shot in the back, the bullet going straight through his heart. He was dead before his body struck the ground.

The routine that followed was like the numbing flow of a long, tired dream for Sandford Courtney. Dully, he walked the endless miles out of the woods to report the tragedy to Forest Ranger Halsey Page. The State Police were notified and Deputy Sheriff Charles Downey and George Mans of Speculator went with Dr. J. B. Van Urk to bring out the body. An investigation at the scene of the shooting was begun.

The inquest at the Hamilton County jail proceeded far into the night. Coroner John Sullivan of Long Lake took charge immediately after the body was brought out of the woods.

The verdict was "accidental death." There was no evidence of criminal negligence, the coroner stated, "except for carelessness on the part of the deceased, who was a veteran hunter and woodsman."

"Lamphier, who had resided in Lake Pleasant and vicinity practically all his life, was popular there," the newspapers told their readers. "He was considered an expert woodsman. The survivors include his wife and two small children . . ."

The veteran guide and hunter, Sanford Courtney, had an abhorrence of hunting to his dying day.

ADIRONDACK BUSH PILOTS

OMINOUS WORD came out of the woods that bleak November day in 1952. Fifty-six-year-old Forest Ranger Jim Lawrence had suddenly been taken seriously ill. Concern in the mountain villages was wide-spread.

For years, Abe and Louise Pritchard Lawrence's tall, unswervingly straight son, Jim, had been forest ranger at the State Conservation Department's most remote watch station on the shores of West Canada Lake. The location is some twenty-two miles by foot or jogging jeep to the nearest highway. There is no electricity, none of the modern conveniences. A portable radio and shaky telephone line strung through the trees to Speculator are the only connections with the outside world.

Stalwart Jim Lawrence was returning through the woods from an inspection of South Canada Lake country that Friday afternoon. A half-mile from his headquarters, he coughed and felt a sharp pain deep inside. He was able to eat little that evening and pain racked his strong muscular body throughout the night.

When his condition showed little improvement the following day, Dorothy Alberts Lawrence knew what to do. A request went over the uncertain single telephone wire to Clyde Elliott, seaplane owner and pilot at Speculator, to fly in and take her husband to Dr. Rollin Fiero in the village. Forest Ranger Halsey Page was notified and it was his decision that Lawrence must be removed that night.

One major obstacle existed. The weather was bad. Several inches of treacherous white snow covered the frigid ground. Foggy dusk had already fallen, and snow swept from cloudy skies. With ceiling zero, a plane flight was impossible.

Halsey Page martialed his forces. Seasonal Ranger Robert

Barton was directed to take his three-man trail-maintenance crew over the eight rough miles from Cedar Lakes to West Canada. T. F. Clark, Jr. at West Canada was notified to stand by. Page himself, with Ranger Ed Broland, started by jeep for Cedar Lakes to receive the stretcher-borne patient when the rangers bore their heavy burden down the rugged mountain trail.

The plan went awry when Barton contacted Halsey Page at Cedar Lakes. The ailing Lawrence was in no condition to be carried out of the woods, he said. With stark determination, Page and Broland accomplished the first desperate jeep drive ever made over the narrow foot-trail. When further progress proved impossible, they walked the last three miles through knee-deep snow to find Lawrence on his stomach, propped up on pillows and crosswise on the bed, a position that caused him less pain.

Hope rose when Page and Broland noted that the weather was beginning to clear at 3 A.M. The skies were momentarily clear at Speculator, too, reported Clyde Elliott over the twenty-two-mile telephone line.

Clyde had to winch his plane out of the hangar. He left his jeep lights shining on the lake to guide him back to home port. As the plane headed northward in the darkness, the bush pilot ran into a snowstorm over Pillsbury Mountain and had to detour by way of Spruce Mountain. The faint, glimmering beams of flashlights held by Halsey Page and Bob Barton, seated atop the Lawrence cabin, guided him to a successful landing on the choppy waves of the lake.

Assisted by two men, Jim Lawrence walked to the plane. Ten minutes later, the weather had closed in once more.

When the patient reached Speculator, Dr. Fiero's hasty inspection told that hospitalization was required. In one short hour, Clyde Elliott drove his automobile the fifty-four miles to Amsterdam, where an emergency operation for ruptured ulcer was performed by Dr. C. A. Spence.

Twelve days passed and Jim Lawrence was back on his feet,

although he would not be able to work until Christmas. A mountain man's bravery had saved the forest ranger's life.

Jim recovered first rate. Four years later, hikers on the trail from Cedar to West Canada Lake were amazed to find an improvised log bridge across Mud Lake stream. The top logs were thirty-two feet long and eight feet above the water. Forest-wise Ranger Jim Lawrence, at sixty-two years of age, had built the bridge alone and with his own muscular arms and powerfully masterful hands.

Some months later, Jim Lawrence and Clyde Elliott were invited to appear on the Columbia Broadcasting System's national television "Wheel of Fortune" program. Full recognition of the flier's daring errand of mercy was accorded and awards were bestowed.

Although made under unusually perilous conditions, the dramatic flight was not entirely new to Clyde. A bush pilot in the mountains is called for many services other than his usual stock and trade of carrying hunters and fishermen to the back-country lakes.

Five years earlier, Clyde had been summoned to pick up Forest Ranger Ernie Ovitt, who had severed an artery in his arm with an axe. Fallen trees had cut the telephone line to West Canada at the time, and Ernie had to hike to Cedar Lake before the pilot could be reached.

There have been several highly capable pilots in Hamilton County, including Harold Scott and Matthew (Windy) Windhousen of Inlet, and Herb Helms of Long Lake. But somehow, Clyde Elliott's location at Speculator seems to place him in direct line for most of the calls.

One summer day in 1955, William Beebe on the Pillsbury Mountain fire lookout spotted a telltale trace of smoke over Long Pond. Beebe radioed Ranger Halsey Page, who would direct the fight against the blaze. Fifteen minutes later, Halsey and Clyde Elliott were reconnoitering the area from Clyde's plane. By air, the location was only minutes from Speculator while ground distance over rugged terrain was twelve. The trip on foot would have taken hours.

That evening, twenty men were flown into the endangered territory. Hundreds of pounds of equipment went along. Throughout the night, the firefighters battled the blaze. With the first light of dawn, Elliott was in the air ferrying nine and a half hours of steady flying. He delivered eight thousand feet of hose, three gasoline pumps, over two hundred gallons of gasoline, and replacements for the fatigued firefighters.

Page directed the Speculator bush pilot to bring in six more men to increase his crew to twenty-four the following day. The seasoned bush pilot, Windy Windhousen, was summoned to help.

Halsey Page estimated that quick action resulted in only a thousand dollars worth of State-owned timber being destroyed.

The veteran flier, Clyde Elliott, has curtailed the number of flights he makes into the wilderness these days, but other pilots are plying the mountain routes. Bush piloting has become an important part of modern Adirondack life.

MOUNTAIN FOLKS

It is early evening in the Central Adirondacks. In a blaze of glory, the sun paints the sky with the warmest of colors—red and orange and pinks and purples—and sends a path of lingering scarlet across the surface of the lake. Its promise completed of another triumphant day to follow, the flaming orb sinks silently behind the uneven, tree-studded horizon and into the celestial beyond.

The silvery, long-enduring mountain twilight deepens into shadowed dusk. One by one, the distant mountains fade into the tremulous softness of approaching night. The first winking stars appear.

Soon, cool, refreshing air will drift lazily down the mountainsides. Perhaps, the gleam of northern lights will frame the distant peaks in silken whiteness, and a liquid moon will rise to bathe the scene in mellow light.

Here, in the mountain heartland, beneficent nature assumes a vivid, plaintive beauty, haunting in quality, spiritual in import.

And the people who dwell among these mountains? Surely, none can have failed to have assimilated much of the nobility of their surroundings; for people are places and places are people in an exchange of characteristics that make them oftentimes as one. Character is molded by environment, as by progenitors, in a relationship that forges a fulsome bond.

It was the lure of the wilderness that brought the first white settlers to the mountains' fastness. Solid American stock was their heritage. Cruel hardship was their lot.

Hunting and trapping became the first occupations of the mountain residents. The meat of the forest animals was the mainstay of the family's larder. Deerskin hides were sold to be made into leather. The fur of the fox, the mink, and the sable brought small amounts of needed cash. With the clearing of a few small acres, grain and potatoes were sown, and those hardier crops that the short growing season of the high elevation would permit. The first primitive farming had begun.

While other sections of the country developed and prospered, the mountain regions were left in isolation. The canals and railroads that brought wealth-producing commerce to the growing nation were often projected but never materialized. The boulder-filled roads remained primitive, as help from any but local government was withheld. It was expensive to get crops and woodland products to market. It was impossible to compete with the produce of lusher lands. For years, the resourceful mountain people were dependent on themselves alone.

Such living breeds a hardy type. Bravery was a prime requirement. Independence was an abject need. Self-reliance became a prime characteristic.

"Yes," the veteran guide Pants Lawrence used to say, in the midst of a cold and snow-filled mountain January, "there are two seasons up here—winter and August. There are some drawbacks to this country. There's six weeks of poor sleighing every year."

Pants, who perhaps typified the mountain mode of living more than most, was demonstrating the attitude of his people toward the hardship that forever was their lot.

Mountain residents ultimately found a way to capitalize on their winter weather as over-stated by the irrepressible Pants. This new-fangled business of winter recreation was barely beginning to catch the public fancy when the people at Speculator started to build the finest of skiing centers. Frankly initiated as a means of providing gainful living to the people in winter, the Oak Mountain Ski Center has become an attraction for people all over the northeast.

Mountain people are like that. Unbelievable ingenuity has been cultivated by these stolid folk under pain of failure to survive. These deeply-ingrained and hard-earned traits remain to characterize the mountain inhabitants of today.

The Adirondacks, with their intrinsic, haunting beauty, offer much to the city visitor, but the final fulfillment comes in knowing those people who live permanently here.

They are friendly, cooperative, congenial people, with an innate kindness and deep human understanding. In them, is a liking for their fellow man. Yet a barrier to complete understanding will at first exist.

The visitor who would know the mountain people must first have an inner feeling for nature's woodlands. If he holds a sacredness for the woodsman's creed, if he can suffer and love and not show these deepest of emotions, then he can become their friend. Greediness, untruthfulness or unfair dealings need occur but once and the door to friendship is forever barred.

When friendship has been gained, a whole new life will have

opened, as mysteriously as though some ancient forest genie had waved a magic wand.

One must never become overly familiar. Never slap a mountain man on the back. Such sign of mutual understanding in other localities can be a signal of a patronizing attitude in the mountains. One must tailor his customs and mind his manners.

To know a mountain resident is to respect his thinking. To live beside him is to respect one's native land. For here, where conditions have caused the hand of the past to reach so deeply into the present, is the true American found at his finest. And the feeling persists that these are the type of people that have helped make America great.